# When You Both Go to Work

The two-paycheck lifestyle is fast becoming the dominant trend in the American family. As growing numbers of women pursue careers—and as others feel pressed by economic necessity to take outside jobs—more and more husbands and wives are facing the special set of problems and rewards being a two-paycheck family brings.

Many of these working couples, like journalists Louis and Kay Moore, are Christians who want church to be an important part of their lives. But many are discovering that staying active in church is not easy for them. They have difficulty finding their niche in churches whose activities are scheduled for the more traditional one-paycheck households. They want to participate in church programs, but they feel pulled by the conflicting demands on their time and energies. And many meet with criticism and condemnation from other Christians, whose love and support they desperately need.

To find out just how Christian couples are coping with these conflicts, and to see how these couples manage to include church in their hectic schedules, the Moores interviewed dozens of working couples from ten different denominations. They found that the difficulties they themselves had experienced in juggling work, home, and church responsibilities were not unique. But they also found many husbands and wives who had developed creative strategies for keeping their sanity while managing to be productive workers, good housekeepers, loving parents, and committed church members. In this book the Moores share what they have learned from these couples and from their own experience about setting priorities, budgeting time, learning when to say no (and when to say yes), and handling criticism lovingly.

Is there a place in the church for two-paycheck families? Louis and Kay Moore answer yes! They believe the dual-career family needs the church, and that the church needs them, too.

(Continued on back flap)

# When You Both Go to Work

# When You Both Go to Work

How Two-Paycheck Families
Can Stay Active in the Church

# Louis & Kay Moore

**WORD BOOKS**
PUBLISHER
WACO, TEXAS

*To Matthew,*
*who gave us the*
*challenge.*

# Contents

Foreword—Ken Chafin   9
Acknowledgments   11
1. Church: Support or Impediment?   13
2. Why Bother with Church, Anyway?   27
3. Some Biblical Dimensions   46
4. Putting First Things First   70
5. Learning to Say No   88
6. Finding the Right Church for You   105
7. What If Your Best Friend Disagrees?   126
8. Juggling Your Act   146
9. Fathers: A Crucial Factor   170
10. Hope for the Future   185
    Notes   201

# Foreword

*When You Both Go to Work* is a desperately needed book. For a variety of reasons there is an increasing number of women who are working outside the home. But this does not mean these two-paycheck couples are any less interested in building strong marriages and healthy families or are moving away from their faith. At the same time, very little thinking has been done by most couples as to how to manage the goals and priorities of life in a two-paycheck family. And the church as a whole has not been sensitive to their needs. Both the couples involved in a two-paycheck family and the church and her leaders need the insight of this book.

Louis and Kay Moore are certainly the right couple to write it. I had observed these two people professionally long before I knew them personally. Week by week I admired their highly developed skills as writers in the articles they wrote for the *Houston Chronicle*, Texas's largest daily newspaper.

I've since come to know them in a friendship relationship and have developed an appreciation for the persons behind the bylines. They are exciting and warm human beings who give a high priority to their marriage, are deeply serious about being good parents, and are persons who love the church and give it a place of importance in their lives.

The book is both practical and probing. It deals honestly with feelings, attitudes, criticism, and problems without being defensive or negative. It deals practically, but never simplistically, with everything from finding a church home to finding time to clean the house.

The book is intensely interesting because the lives of

real people are woven into it. Louis and Kay are the primary couple, and this gives the book an autobiographical feel. The authors did enough in-depth interviews with other two-paycheck families from every segment of society to rescue the book from any danger of narrowness. They have woven experiences, insights, interviews, and applications in a very readable manner.

The book has a solid feel about it. This comes partly from the fact that the authors are very clear about their assumptions and practices. They have very settled convictions about marriage, parenting, and God in their lives. This solidity also comes from the constant referral to the Bible and the sensitive interpretations of the texts which relate to their theme.

This is a *must* book for every individual who is part of a two-paycheck family. Its honesty and awareness, coupled with its practical insights, will provide handles for enriching every life.

I'd like to put the book on the required reading list for all Christian communicators. As I read the manuscript, I found myself sensitized to my own need to become an encourager, equipper, and friend to all the people in the circle of my responsibility who are a part of a two-paycheck family.

KEN CHAFIN
February, 1982

# Acknowledgments

This book depends heavily on interviews with the thirty-six churchgoing two-paycheck couples who gave up their Sunday afternoons to talk with us about their lives. Without their input, we would still be floundering in our turmoil, thinking surely we were the only such couple on earth struggling to find a church that would affirm our lifestyle. The names used herein are their actual ones, except in the case of six couples who requested pseudonymns be assigned to them.

We could not complete our task here without expressing gratitude to the management of the *Houston Chronicle*, who took a then-unorthodox step in hiring us as a married couple a decade ago, and who have undergirded us as a two-paycheck team for all the years hence. We feel our *Chronicle* editors are sterling examples of how employers can be sensitive to the family needs of those who work for them.

We are deeply indebted to the staff of Word Books, who proved to be genuine friends as well as editors and facilitators for this project. Special mention goes to Floyd Thatcher, for his splendid supervision; Anne Christian Buchanan, for her judicious and brilliant editing; and Ernest Owen and Debi Klingsporn for their thoughtful advice.

We also owe much to Matthew's grandmother, Grace Moore, for countless hours of child care she provided to allow us to do our research.

And a final word of thanks to our new daughter, Catharine Louisa, for delaying her arrival into this world until six days after our writing deadline for this book had passed.

LOUIS AND KAY MOORE
February 14, 1982

# 1. Church: Support or Impediment?

Kay, who usually does not engage in marathon telephone conversations, talked longer than usual that Sunday afternoon. I assumed it was because we had been absent from church that morning and Kay's friend Margie was giving her an extra-detailed briefing on the litany of the church parties, meetings, and illnesses that were announced in Sunday school. Even though Kay's lunch got colder by the minute because of the lengthy call, I felt the conversation was healthy because it would give Kay a sense of being wanted and missed.

But the look on my wife's face as she hung up the phone and sat down to eat was anything but cheerful.

"Did I really hear her correctly?" she finally sputtered after a long silence. "Margie told me that the Sunday school class had a special prayer this morning that Barbara Mahoney would stay home permanently with her new baby and not follow my example of returning to work and leaving a small child."

The savory chicken and rice casserole I had been devouring suddenly went flat on my taste buds and lost its appeal. The conversation Kay had just relayed represented more than just idle chatter between friends. It seemed to cap a growing surge of insensitivity that we had experienced among fellow church members since Kay resumed her job as a newspaper reporter three months earlier. She had been home on a year's maternity leave with our son Matthew, and we felt good about our decision to become a two-paycheck family again.

But a series of events, culminating in this latest comment that the Sunday school class was "praying" for a friend in a similar situation, had made Kay and me take a serious look at our church involvement, and at whether our two-paycheck lifestyle was actually meant to survive in a contemporary church situation.

Kay's return to work was no fly-by-night decision, but was in keeping with a plan we had mapped out as early as our courtship days. Long before our wedding in August, 1969, we knew that our union would be a two-paycheck one and that our family life, in whatever form it took down the years, would see both of us working full-time outside the home.

Kay was committed from the time she was eleven to a career in writing. To her, it was a "calling," just as real as any a pulpit minister or a missionary could feel. In later years, she would hang a typed scripture verse on her desk that she seemed to feel represented her mission in life. It was from John 18:37 and read, "For this I was born, and for this I have come into the world, to bear witness to the truth. Every one who is of the truth hears my voice." It was Christ's testimony before Pilate, but Kay felt it pretty well summed up her purpose in terms of her writing career.

By the time I was in college, I was weaving together my earlier interests in writing and ministry into a vocation of religious journalism. Kay and I met while working on the student newspaper at Baylor University. Its advisers insisted on running the newspaper in a professional manner, so that young journalists could get an accurate taste of what was in store for them in the work world. Since Kay and I fell in love in such a setting, each of us had a glimpse from the beginning of what demands our careers would place on us. I was as ambitious for her as she was for me, and we were willing to meet the challenge.

Something else we agreed on at an early stage in our relationship was that the church would always be an important part of our married life. Both of us had been reared in churchgoing families, as Southern Baptists. Our personal faith was important to each of us. We promised ourselves that as a married couple, and later as parents, we would be actively involved in church, teach Sunday school, and rear any eventual children in a home where church attendance and participation were a way of life.

These needs were even cemented in our wedding vows. Our dear and trusted friend, counselor, and professor, Dr. Glenn Hilburn, of Baylor's religion faculty, who performed our ceremony, admonished us that in our marriage, our first responsibility was to God, our second was to each other, our third was to our children, and our fourth to our professions. We left the church on our wedding day convinced we could carry out our plan and have it all—marriage, children, careers, and a deep spiritual life and commitment to a church.

During our first childless years of marriage, it was difficult enough to do the juggling act that being a two-paycheck family requires and still be churchgoers. We both held full-time newspaper jobs and found it hard to limit our work week to forty hours; it was a period of our lives when getting a foothold on the career ladder was important. We wanted to spend significant amounts of time together, and we wanted to make close friends. It was hard to sandwich in the extra committee meetings, phone calls, visitation and lesson preparation that were expected of church workers. But we had no children and lived in an apartment that needed only minimal care, so teaching a Sunday school class became our main extracurricular activity. We enjoyed taking our college student class members on retreats, giving them parties, and welcoming them into our home.

## A Child Complicates the Plan

But when our son, a carefully-planned-for and much-wanted child, was born and Kay returned to work, we discovered our plan was much more difficult to execute than we had ever imagined. By that time, we had moved into a house, which required more upkeep than had our virtually maintenance-free apartment. Time was at a premium. It seemed to take all our energies just to juggle two jobs, maintain a house, continue building a healthy marriage, spend effective time with our son, and negotiate all the new demands—such as finding good day care and making contingency arrangements for a sick child—that were suddenly thrust upon us. Home and time together as a family suddenly became like a "third career."

To our surprise, the church became almost impossible to fit into our lifestyle. The most we could possibly manage seemed to be putting in an appearance for Sunday morning worship. We wanted to continue to build warm, close ties with our friends at church. We wanted to teach Sunday school. We wanted to be on committees. We wanted to be as active as ever.

But we soon discovered that our church was not organized for two-paycheck families, and particularly not for working parents. Its programs were still set up for the traditional husband-at-work, wife-at-home marriage. And we discovered that our expectations for being active were out of touch with the amount of time we could give and still maintain a decent home life.

Kay suddenly found herself missing out on social activities with her group of church friends, who were all members with young children at home, because women's socials were always scheduled for the daytime with a nursery provided for the children. The rare events that were scheduled at night, such as missionary circle meetings, also posed a problem. It seemed to Kay that many of the women in attendance looked on these meetings as a "mother's night out" away from husband and children, as well as an opportunity for Bible study or missions emphasis. But the working woman, who has been away from home and family all day, even more seriously needs a mother's night "in"—at home. It was hard to identify with these women's need to escape, since the working woman has so little time to spend with her children. So, much to our distress, such church activities suddenly began to fall by the wayside.

As a couple, we also found it next to impossible to attend church social activities at night, because events usually were planned on weeknights when we were both exhausted from a day of working outside the home. Saturday night would have been a much more acceptable "party" night for us, after we had a day of breathing space from the office. But we found that our church hesitated to schedule social events on Saturday nights for fear that the faithful would sleep in and not be in the pews on Sunday mornings. We found that few people could understand our plight, because week-night parties were not considered a problem by one-paycheck couples, where one member of the team—usually the wife—kept the home fires burning during the day. So we soon found ourselves cut off from church fellowship that was important to us.

## Cutting into Parenting Time

Teaching a Sunday school class also became an impossibility. Our church leaned heavily on Sunday school teachers to attend midweek teachers' meetings and regular visitation programs. For us, each additional evening out of the week meant more time away from home and Matthew, when we'd already been gone from him all day. Furthermore, staying in church nurseries past his bedtime several nights a week only complicated the problem of rousing a sleepy-headed child in the mornings. Children need to be in bed at an early hour, and sleep uninterrupted, so they can adjust to early rising schedules. Even if Matthew fell asleep while in the care of a church nursery, we felt that rousting him from slumber to carry him home would be doing him a disservice.

In many ways, we felt our church was requiring us to cut into our "prime-time parenting"; this seemed a big contradiction for an institution which emphasized family togetherness and family life. Church leaders suggested to us what they felt was a compromise: "OK, it's all right if just one of you comes to teachers' meetings, just as long as your family is represented." But for us, this seemed an untenable solution. We felt that Matthew needed both parents—not just one—at home on workday evenings, instead of one parent bounding off regularly for weeknight church events.

For the two-paycheck family, just getting up for Sunday morning worship seemed a sacrifice—even if we hadn't partied the night before. Saturdays were our main errand days. They were a rat race of packing everything in, with groceries to buy, a house to clean, a yard to mow, and myriads of other projects that wives without outside jobs apportion out on weekdays to lighten their Saturday loads. Sundays were often the only real "family day" that we had.

Another unexpected problem we encountered was Matthew's involvement in church programs—particularly Vacation Bible School, the annual summertime event that many denominations schedule for their youngsters. Churches usually hold these programs on weekday mornings for one or two weeks out of the year in an effort to teach Bible truths in a fun atmosphere conducive to learning. Bible School was a summertime "staple" for both Kay and me during our childhoods; it was as much a part of summer and growing up as were ice cream and mud pies and swimming lessons. We yearned to have Matthew participate just as we had.

But again, it seemed that such activities for children were planned without working parents in mind. Bible School ended for the youngsters at one o'clock in the afternoon;

we did not get off work until five. It was impossible for us, during our workday, to leave our jobs, drive the considerable distance to our church, pick up Matthew, and deposit him at his nursery. We asked our church to consider providing an extended child care service for those children in Matthew's situation who needed a place to stay until five o'clock, when their parents got off work. As an alternative, we asked if they could arrange transportation for Matthew to his nursery school after the Bible School session was over. But they gave neither plan serious consideration. Again, it seemed that the two-paycheck family was left on the fringes.

## The Biggest Problem—Others' Opinions

But the biggest problem we encountered as a two paycheck family in the church was something totally unexpected. It was the total lack of emotional support we received from the institution that we hoped would yield the most affirmation in times of crisis and change.

Even though her plans to work were known well before she went on maternity leave, Kay's friends in our couples Sunday school class were openly critical when the day came for her to return to her job. The idea of a woman with a small child going back to work was uncomfortable for them, and several women in the class made unkind, unsolicited remarks. No one seemed aware that Kay craved affirmation during this shift from home to work; their main response seemed to be a chorus of "how could you?" about leaving our son in a commercial day-care center, which was our carefully weighed choice for his care.

If our family had undergone a stressful period due to illness, death in the family, or financial reversal, we felt that these same friends would have rallied around us with their prayers, with offers to help, with encouraging words and supportive comments. But instead of recognizing Kay's return to the job market as a major life change that was bound to create tensions—no matter how comfortable we were with the decision—our church friends created an additional impediment by their negative, naysaying attitudes. We were not asking anyone to agree with our decision or to model our choice. But even a nebulous, noncommittal comment such as, "Gee, it must be really tough for you," or "I admire your willingness to try to balance home and work," would have helped ease us over a few rough spots in those first few days of change.

We felt that events were on the same plane as when a friend announced recently that she was moving out of the apartment she had shared with her boyfriend for the past year. As she told us of her decision, her eyes were puffy from crying and her pain in taking this action was obvious.

It would have been very easy for us to seize this opportunity to lecture or sermonize about how wrong we felt she was to live with him in the first place. Our personal bias is against unmarried couples cohabiting. But the last thing this heartbroken girl needed was our unsolicited opinions. The thing she needed most was to know that her friends would continue being her friends, and that they believed in her, no matter what. A simple remark to her like, "I'm sure this must be a very difficult time for you," did not compromise our beliefs, and it extended a much-needed hand of friendship.

Kay's conversation that Sunday afternoon with Margie, about the class member who had just had a baby and was trying to decide if and when to return to the job market, seemed to be the last straw as far as our frustrations were concerned. Barbara, the friend in question, had been a public school teacher before her daughter was born. She had always been a woman Kay could identify with because Barbara, unlike the other women in the class, seemed very career-oriented and had a sense of mission about her work. During Barbara's pregnancy, she had discussed her future plans with Kay. Kay sensed in Barbara that she had found a "soul sister" who had caught a vision of blending career and family life; for Barbara, teaching was more than "just a job"; it was something she felt called to do and sorely needed for personal fulfillment.

But as Barbara pondered out loud about the decision she was considering, the same Sunday school class members who had responded negatively to Kay's choice of going back to work pounced even more firmly on Barbara. By having a class prayer that Barbara would not yield to her career desires and would stay home permanently, these church members seemed to be making a firm statement that the two-paycheck lifestyle was unacceptable in a church setting.

## An Either/Or Situation

For the first time, we began to wonder whether we were faced with an either/or situation. Should we continue our lifestyle and be forever discouraged about church? Or should we abandon our long-held plan and become a one-paycheck family again, so we would have time to be more actively involved in our congregation as well as to ensure the approval of our friends? There were points at which we seriously considered each option. But we knew how much the church meant to our lives. And we still felt Kay deserved a career as much as I did.

To help answer our dilemma, we began searching through some of the two-paycheck-family books that had begun flooding the market, with all their lists of how-tos. There was plenty of advice on selecting day-care centers, coping with bosses, keeping marriage sexually exciting, handling work/home conflicts, and spending quality time with children—matters we'd already dealt with. But written materials seemed to abysmally lack advice about how working couples can stay active in their churches. The books either left out the subject entirely, or made only a passing mention of church under "extracurricular activities"—along with advice on how to work in Kiwanis clubs and bridge groups.

This seemed hardly the proper category for something as meaningful as the church. No body of literature seemed to exist on dealing with what was fast becoming the biggest stumbling block to our two-paycheck game plan—how to keep the church a part of our lives.

We looked to our professional friends for answers, and again found little help. Most of our friends at work who had successful two-paycheck lifestyles did not include the church in their marriage, either because they simply did not believe church was important, because they felt alienated from the church, or because they wanted to attend but simply could not work it in. Looking about us at other individuals in the pew, we saw mostly one-paycheck families. It seemed that those who remained vital and active in the church were those who were not having to cope with the stresses of the two-paycheck lifestyle. In the pulpit were few role models either. The clergy seemed to be the last frontier for working wives. Only in the past few years has it been considered "acceptable" for pastors' wives to seek outside employment other than in church volunteer work. The only church leaders who seemed at all sensitive to our plight were those whose wives had experimented on a limited basis with outside jobs and knew firsthand of the difficulties we were encountering.

## Not a Passing Fad

Were we fighting a losing battle? It seemed that way. But statistics told us we were not alone. The two-paycheck family is not a fad that will drop by the wayside as soon as women "get it out of their systems" as some critics claim. It is fast becoming the dominant lifestyle in the United States.

Women make up about 40 percent of the labor force,[1] and about half of those are married. The number of women in the labor force, 37.0 million in 1975, is projected to rise by 11.6 million by 1990, an increase of 1.8 percent per year.[2]

Nearly half of all mothers of preschoolers in the United States work at jobs outside the home. About 57 percent of the mothers with children under the age of eighteen are working; ten years ago the percentage was only 42 percent.[3] One in five of these mothers is a single parent,[4] but the majority are married women with working husbands.

Wives return to work for economic security in times of double-digit inflation and shrinking dollars overseas. And more and more young women today are leaving college, as Kay did, with the commitment to both a career and family. In 1980, the median age of women not in the labor force was nearly fifty-two years, compared with slightly over forty-five in 1970.[5] Some women are developing part-time jobs at home to pay the bills and provide creative outlets and a sense of worth they feel they need. And some of these part-time jobs are turning into full-time careers! Affirmative action plans have brought blue-collar and white-collar working women new advances and status. Some women are reentering outside employment after time out to rear families; others are returning because of some life crisis, such as divorce or widowhood. Women now have an unprecedented number of options to create full, varied, and meaningful lives—including, of course, choosing to remain full-time homemakers, with no outside employment, if that is what they feel called to do. Our place here is certainly not to advocate one lifestyle over another, but to simply state why we chose ours and to emphasize that today it is just that—a matter of choice.

Quite obviously, like every other institution in our society, churches must eventually come face to face with the needs of two-paycheck families—ours and everyone else's. Can they really afford not to? For with the return of women to the work force, much of the volunteer labor churches have relied on for years to conduct activities such as local missionary work, vacation church schools, bazaars and crafts fairs, outreach, and mailings—to name a few—will instead be opting for paying jobs in the secular marketplace. To blindly refuse to recognize the cultural shifts that are affecting families today will ultimately leave the church without the feet and hands on which it has depended for years to do its work. Furthermore, it will alienate loyal members who, by choice or by necessity, join the ranks of the two-paycheck families.

Failing to acknowledge the shift toward two-paycheck families will also leave the church without influence in the soon-to-be dominant lifestyle in this country. Will the churches abandon these couples because their way of life does not fit the traditional mold? If so, churches may some-day, belatedly, have to hustle to develop new outreach ministries to this segment of society, in the same way churches in the 1970s rushed to create new ministries to divorced persons—years after divorce became a major factor in our society.

## Finally, Some Answers

With all these facts in mind, we decided to go it alone and search out other church-oriented, two-paycheck families who could serve as our models and help shape our thinking. In the five years since that troubling Sunday afternoon phone call, we've met a number of couples who have succeeded in building successful, stable two-paycheck marriages and fully-active, meaningful church relationships. Locating these people has been like a breath of fresh air on a stuffy August day; they have given hope and inspiration to us.

We interviewed thirty-six couples in which both husband and wife hold full-time jobs, and who also consider themselves active in their local congregations. These were couples from every economic bracket—from blue-collar working spouses who were "just scraping by" to a husband and wife who each earned an income in the six-figure category. Accordingly, the women who worked outside the home fit into a wide range of categories—from women who considered themselves to be "only helping out" until their husbands overcame a financial reversal, to women who, like Kay, felt their work fulfilled a personal mission. The couples represented every major Christian denomination in the country, as well as a few of the smaller groups, because we wanted to see if all churchgoing two-paycheck couples encountered the same problems that we did, or if there were certain problems or benefits characteristic of individual denominations.

The couples we interviewed shared with us in nuts-and-bolts terms how they've set their own priorities and worked out compromises to get the most from their church activities without sacrificing family life. They showed us how to say no to church programs we didn't have time for, without losing standing among church friends. They showed us how to handle those in the church and elsewhere who feel threatened by this new but rapidly growing model for home life, and how to lobby with churches for more flexibility in schedules of activities. They showed us how to select a church that is right for working couples and how to act as consumers to help the clergy become more aware of changing lifestyles, as well as introducing us to some creative and enlightened churches that have already responded to this need and are actively helping two-paycheck couples. They gave us a myriad of useful tips on how they manage their personal time to make room for church events. And, perhaps most importantly, they shared with us a number of compelling reasons why they believe church is worth the extra effort a two-paycheck family must put forth to arrive in the pew after a barn-burner of a week.

Out of these discussions, and out of our own trial-and-error experimentation, we've hammered out a plan for us, which we'll share in these pages. We don't claim that our plan has all the answers; we are still learning and testing and refining our lifestyle. Nor has it been enacted without some heartache. Finding a workable answer for our family has meant changing congregations several times. (We now attend a church that has a unique Friday night worship service as an alternative to Sunday morning.)

Our plan has its weaknesses, just as any lifestyle has its problems. And ours is certainly not the perfect two-paycheck marriage. Like all marriages, it is not immune to troubles. But it does work, and we think it works well. We believe we've found a good way to blend the church into our complex day-to-day life, and we've done enough reflecting and probing to believe it also can work for others.

We believe two-paycheck families need the church, and that the church needs them. In this book we will explore dozens of ideas that we hope will help working couples find the same happiness and fulfillment through their churches that traditional one-paycheck families have found for years.

# 2. Why Bother with Church, Anyway?

It had been the kind of work week that inspired recurrent thoughts of chunking it all and becoming hermits on a remote island. The unshakeable overcast skies and icy wind—unusual in Houston even for January—seemed to set a dour tone for the entire five days. Traffic snarls due to the weather complicated getting to and from downtown. At the office, flu diminished the ranks of employees, and those who slipped by the bug and struggled to their jobs seemed almost to envy the absent workers. Everyone felt listless and irritable.

My personal work schedule that week seemed to be totally guided by Murphy's Law: "Whatever can go wrong, will." I was slated to interview a rabbi for my lead story in the coming weekend's religion section of the *Houston Chronicle.* Just as I was leaving for the appointment, the rabbi's secretary called to say that the rabbi, too, had succumbed to the flu and wanted to postpone our meeting for two weeks. I had to pound the pavement quickly to find another story to take its place.

I completed all my interviews just in time to join in the midweek office uproar over yet another computer breakdown. The word processing system that has replaced typewriters, paper, and linotype machines and has thoroughly streamlined newspaper production had stalled, just as re-

porters were readying their stories for the fat weekend edi-
tion of the *Chronicle*. I could feel the tension climbing rapidly as deadlines neared with my stories unfinished. By
the time I corrected the last page proof on my section that
Friday afternoon, I felt as though my nerves were stretched
tissue thin.

Meanwhile, Kay had undergone her share of troubles,
too. Since we work for the same newspaper, with offices
only a few steps away in the same building, we share the
same business-wide problems. The malfunctioning computer also had thrown a monkey wrench into her work
week, destroying parts of a story she was writing as the
system "crashed." What's worse, an editor had cancelled
one of her key projects in midweek after learning that another department of the paper was writing on the same
subject. Kay was demolished over the turn of events.

As five o'clock Friday approached, and we met to check
our signals for the evening, I instantly detected from Kay's
tired eyes and defeated look that we both had the same
thought: forego our regular Friday night worship service
at church that week, pick up Matthew from his school,
and retreat home for a cup of hot cocoa and a TV movie.
The special Friday service, designed for couples like us who
need a weekly worship experience but prefer to reserve
Sunday as a family day, solves a critical need for our two-
paycheck family. On most weeks, the dinner from the
church kitchen preceding the service is enough to revive
our weariness and allow us to reframe our thoughts to prepare for worship. But on this particular Friday night, Kay
and I both agreed that even a lobster meal at Tony's, the
most expensive restaurant in town, could not jar us from
our fatigue and resignation enough to put us in a worshipful
mood. Surely God would affirm that we deserved the rest.

Despite our misgivings, however, the Moore family, pro-
pelled by something we were hard-pressed to explain,
pulled into the church's parking lot at the usual time. No
matter how many excuses we invented, none seemed to

justify backing out of our Friday night church commitment. Perhaps we held some tacit hope that church would offer a bright spot to resurrect the week from a total wasteland and allow it to close on a happier note. Perhaps we were simply tempted by the church's low-cost meal that promised to be more nourishing than what we would get at a fast-food stop on the way home.

Whatever our reasons, almost from the moment we stepped in the door, we were glad we came. The warmth of a relaxed conversation with a group of intimate friends seated around the church dinner table was in sharp contrast to the chilly drizzle that fell outside. A fellow church member who had recognized Kay's byline on a recent newspaper story pulled her aside and complimented her on the article. This note of encouragement provided a touch of warmth and affirmation that Kay sorely needed after a "losing" week.

Once in the church sanctuary, the stirring chords of familiar old hymns seemed themselves a comfort and reassurance. Even though our minds drifted more than the normal amount, we still caught a few morsels from the pastor's sermon on facing life with a sense of triumph (from Romans 8:26–28). And a phrase from the closing prayer reminded us that, despite a discouraging week at work, we could count many blessings: sound health, safety to and from work, talents and skills that enable us to provide for our family. Though we came to church feeling distracted and estranged, we left with a sense of God's enveloping love that can permeate even the most dismal life crisis. We chided ourselves as we realized how close we had come to skipping church that night and missing out on so much. Our attitudes had changed from one of defeat to one that echoed the familiar Bible verse: "I was glad when they said unto me, Let us go into the house of the Lord" (Ps. 122:1, KJV).

Whether they are faced with attending a Friday night service or with the more traditional Sunday morning variety after a harrowing work week, for most two-paycheck couples it is a tremendous effort to include church. Friday night is usually a "collapse" time for most two-paycheck couples, who often act out the scenario of crashing in front of a TV set after a take-out meal like the plan we toyed with after our rough Friday. Saturday usually goes by in a wild flurry of errands, as the couple tries to cram in just about any chore that didn't get done during the week. If they attempt to have a social life, Saturday night is their only chance to leave the kids with a sitter and go out with friends or to a movie, but even that must be curtailed early if they plan to wake in time for church on Sunday. When the alarm clock rings at six the next morning to rouse the family for Sunday school, the bleary-eyed two-paycheck husband and wife wonder what's happened to the "restful" weekend they envisioned all day Friday. A trip to church will tie them up until at least 12:30 P.M., and lunch afterward probably won't end until two. That leaves precious little time to the weekend, especially if their church demands attendance on Sunday night also. Who could blame them for opting to "sleep in" Sunday after Sunday?

Yet, week after week, numerous two-paycheck couples make the same decision we did on that weary Friday night and attend church faithfully, despite a tempting pull to stay at home. The couples we interviewed gave at least eight different, compelling reasons why they "bother" with church.

## It's Always Been There

On some Sunday mornings, Curtis Lengefeld would consider it a luxury if he could wake to an alarm going off at six in the morning. Quite often, he's assigned to work the Saturday graveyard shift at a petroleum plant. That puts him home at 5:00 A.M. Sunday, giving him just enough time to shower off the grime, eat breakfast and brush up on the Sunday school lesson he will teach that morning at a Baptist church near his home. Their schedule might be simplified if Curtis' wife Sandra were home all week to keep the house running, but Sandra is an eighth-grade English teacher at a middle school. She's worked almost non-stop throughout her entire adult life, pausing only briefly for the births of two sons, aged ten and four.

When asked why they include church in their schedules despite a rigorous work arrangement that would tax even the sturdiest person, Sandra replied, "We were both reared in homes where we went to church on Sundays. We never assumed anybody did anything any different than that."

Carol Dinkins, a highly successful lawyer, must make an arduous sacrifice to attend her Lutheran church on Sunday mornings. Recently appointed to a federal post in the U.S. Justice Department, Carol lives in Washington, D.C., on weekdays and commutes halfway across the continent to spend Saturday and Sunday with her family. Meanwhile, her husband Ted leads his own busy life. He's a prominent attorney specializing in estate law, with cases such as the Howard Hughes estate to his credit. They have two school-aged daughters.

The Dinkins' weekend is jam-packed—fuller even than that of most two-paycheck families—because Carol devotes her time to becoming reacquainted with her daughters, whom she has talked with only by long distance telephone from Washington all week. There also are clothes to clean, suitcases to repack, and household arrangements to make. But a must on the Dinkinses' list for the weekend is church—and for the same reasons the Lengefelds cited.

"I grew up in a family where I went to church every Sunday," Carol says. "I would miss church if I didn't go at least once in a while."

Ted views the church and regular church attendance as "an anchor" for life. "Since so much of life these days is transitory, it's good to have some institution that remains unchanging," he says.

When Nora and Jim Bishop Jr. were asked why they attend church despite two hectic careers, their eyes glistened a little as they described nostalgic feelings they associated with church from their youth. The Methodist church where both grew up seemed to symbolize stability, security, and the warmth of childhood. Nora is a registered nurse with frequent weekend call; Jim is a graphics designer. Although she treasures her nonworking weekends as a crucial family time, Nora said she would never consider missing church on the Sunday mornings she is not on duty, largely for the sense of "connectedness" it provides with her childhood.

My mother recently hauled down from her attic a box of old family photos to be divided among my brother, my sister, and me. In the bottom of the box was a yellowed, frayed cradle roll certificate showing that churchgoing had been a part of my life since infancy. The date on it indicated that my mother bundled me up and carried me to church on the very first Sunday she was recovered enough from childbirth to get out of the house. A cradle roll certificate in Kay's family album tells a similar story. Therefore, we could easily identify with couples who gravitate to church on Sunday mornings because it brings back memories of a childhood experience. Whether it involves cookies and juice in Sunday school or the chant of a rosary in High Mass, come Sunday mornings, church inspires a certain sense of "oughtness," based on past experiences, that occurs no matter how frenzied the work week has been. For us, like the couples we interviewed, church has "always been there"—an important grounding for our hectic lives.

## For the Children's Sake

Barbara and Terry Myers actually have a three-paycheck family! Terry works full time for the U.S. Mail Service as a letter carrier. Barbara holds down two part-time jobs that equal one full-time job as a bookkeeper. They are parents of two teenaged daughters and a preschooler.

Terry disapproves of parents who "dump their kids at church and go back to pick them up a few hours later.

We want our children to grow up in the right atmosphere," he says. "We want them to learn to cope with life without having to rely on drugs or alcohol. We want them to be able to look within themselves for resources to cope." For these reasons, the family makes a special effort to attend their Presbyterian church regularly.

At church, the Myers feel, their youngsters will be less likely to hang out with the "wrong crowd." Barbara expressed many a mother's hope that through church activities their youngsters will meet "nice kids" from like-minded homes. She felt she could rest easier in the evenings knowing her children were at the church recreation hall instead of flirting with trouble on a convenience store parking lot.

Cecilia Valdes and Mike Rutledge were not yet married when we talked with them. But the two young medical students had decided one thing: no matter how complicated their lives might be in the future with two demanding careers, church would be an important part of their lives, and any children they might have would be reared in the church. Because of that, they were already actively trying to resolve a potential conflict in their relationship: Mike was reared in a Church of Christ, while Cecilia is Roman Catholic.

A compromise may take them years to hammer out, but Mike vowed that he and Cecilia will reach some agreement about church by the time children arrive. "We don't want our kids reared in a home where the parents go their separate ways to church. It is not going to be any good unless we get involved personally." Said Cecilia, "It has to be something the children see reflected in us, not something they see us doing for them. If you go to church just because of the children and don't live it yourselves, it's fake and the children know it."

In her book, *Crosscurrents: Children, Families and Religion*, Evelyn Kaye writes, "In the liberal, ethical, independent culture of today, religion is often dismissed. But the influence of traditional religious ideas quietly, often invisibly, permeates almost every area of our lives. The majority of Americans were brought up in one or another of the traditional religions, and the values they learned in their church or temple, as well as the customs, rituals and ceremonies, still influence their attitudes and thinking. Americans are among the most religiously aware citizens in the Western world, with more than half the total population belonging to a church."[1] Kaye concludes that much of this church attendance is due to the fact that parents want their children to develop some kind of religious orientation.

The scriptural admonition in Proverbs 22:6: "Train up a child in the way he should go: and when he is old, he will not depart from it" (KJV) was an answer often quoted by numerous two-paycheck couples we interviewed. One mother expressed it this way: "We want our children to develop an ethical code of conduct from the values they learn in the church. If they want to rebel when they get older, at least they will have something to rebel from." Another verse that some parents deemed appropriate to this question was Psalm 144:12: "May our sons in their youth be like plants full grown, our daughters like corner pillars cut for the structure of a palace." They believe that only through regular church attendance can their youngsters be strengthened in the Lord for their adulthood ahead. For many two-paycheck couples, these things ring louder in their ears than does the clanging of the alarm clock on a Sunday morning after a difficult week. Except for the kids, the temptation to merely roll over and go back to sleep would be almost overwhelming.

## For a Special Program

Jean and Charlie Storm consider themselves "corporate gypsies." He is an engineer with an oil company. She is a home economist by training, an entrepreneur by profession. Besides appearing in television commercials and publishing her own books, Jean is a consultant on home decoration and self-improvement. On the Sunday afternoon we interviewed them, the Storms were packing their colorfully-accented contemporary furnishings for the movers to come the next day to ship their belongings to Holland, where both Jean and Charlie would continue their careers.

But the frenzied move had not kept them from attending their Presbyterian church that morning, for farewells with friends and to sing in the church choir just one more time. The choir had been their main drawing card to church on Sunday for four years. "We get involved because of the music program," said Charlie. "Neither of us would be happy without expressing ourselves in music. We both feel fulfilled through our singing. It means more to us than does the sermon or the service."

The Storms had already been checking out via long distance the church prospects in The Hague, and planned to join the American Protestant Church there as soon as they arrived in their new home—possibly even the next Sunday. Kay and I bet that if we had looked in on them across the sea a few weeks after our interview, we would have spotted them already in that church's choir loft.

Fatigue showed in Debbie Lobaugh's face when she opened her door for our interview to begin. Debbie, a Baptist, talked openly about how she struggled out of bed on Sunday mornings, being bone weary from her secretarial job and from trying, with husband Bob's help, to be an adequate housekeeper. Like the Storms, she made the Sunday effort because of the choir—but she was a listener, not a singer. "I can be feeling so low, and hear one choir number and it lifts me up," she said. The worshipful solace of sacred music can be like soothing calamine lotion on a burn or a sting.

The choir director in the church where Kay grew up could deliver more of a sermon through his solos than a preacher could in five messages. Many people often murmured, "Well, I've heard my sermon for the day; let's go home," when this gifted soloist finished his special number. For

many working couples, church music seemed to create a
mood that made the Sunday morning struggle worthwhile.

## To Be with Like-Minded People

Madeleine and Mike Hamm often feel like "Lone Ranger"
Christians in their respective professions. Both Madeleine's
field as a journalist and Mike's as an attorney seem to be
deficient in churchgoers among the ranks. For that reason,
they became involved in a Methodist church three years
ago in hopes of meeting people more like them spiritually.

"I felt like the people that belong to the church are people
I would rather become friends with, because we have more
things in common than do people who do not go to church,"
says Mike. "I'm more comfortable with the values of the
people who attend church."

Adds Madeleine: "People who have a faith in God seem
to be a little happier. They just have something more than
others."

Ken Chafin, the pastor of our church, discussed this in
a sermon. "What do we miss when we're never in church?
We miss seeing the evidence of what God is doing in the
lives of his children."[2]

Obviously, this must have been a magnetic force as far
back as the days of the early Christians. After Christ's death
on the cross, people were as moved by the changed lives
of apostles like Peter as they were by the magnificent story
these men told of seeing Jesus alive and risen from the
dead. How difficult it must have been to realize that this
very man—Peter—who became a shrinking coward during
Jesus' trial before Pilate could have experienced a 180-
degree turnaround in attitude and was now willing to give
his own life to spread Christ's message. Around God's work
in the hearts of people like Peter, the early church was
formed. For these people, the sacrifice was not merely resisting the urge to "sleep in" on Sunday mornings, as it is
with working couples; it involved ridicule, persecution, and

sometimes death. Yet these followers risked all, because they could see Christ's power to change lives.

A prison ministry fellowship at our church, which offers Bible study and a support group for ex-offenders, their friends, and their families, is a beautiful modern-day example of this type of change. Robert Ketchand, an attorney who is one of the founders of this group, said, "When we first started meeting about a year ago, not one person admitted to having ever been in jail, or to being the mother or wife of an inmate. Very few people said a word, and when they did offer a comment, they would always preface it by saying, 'My best friend's son is in prison for drugs,' or would use some other disclaimer. After a few months, when the truth finally came out, the meeting was just one massive crying session. No one could talk about their inmate son or husband without sobbing nonstop. Now, it's just incredible. People share openly and intimately and almost cheerfully with each other. Several people in this group have become Christians. God has really been at work in this group."

Whether we hear stories like Robert's, hear personal testimonies in church, or simply talk about the week's events around the Friday night supper table, we are constantly blessed by hearing—and seeing—what God is doing in the lives of his children. Two-paycheck families like the Hamms, whose work environments often provide little contact with "like-minded people," desperately need a place they can go to see that God is still moving and working in the world.

## To Give Something Back to God

Donna and Harold VanderWeide devote their entire work week "giving" to others. As owners and directors of their own private school, they take care of other people's children. Donna teaches both a morning and afternoon class of kindergarten students.

Yet one of their motivations for getting themselves and their two teenaged children to church on Sunday mornings is to keep giving. Harold serves as an elder, teaches an adult class and is chairman of the Youth Task Force at their Presbyterian church. Donna also is on a variety of church committees and attends adult Sunday school. "We are returning only a small part of what God has given to us," she said. "We really should do more—we have so much."

Getting to church on Sunday morning involves baking cookies every Saturday night by Madeleine and Mike, who are responsible for the visitors' coffee after church. Mike often teaches their adult class in Sunday school, Madeleine helps out with publishing the church newsletter, and both are on the church's evangelism committee. "We just feel like we are extremely blessed with a good life and want to serve others in some way," said Madeleine. "I would rather expend my energies through the church than through something like a social club."

Two-paycheck couples who make church a part of their lives can easily feel that they've expended their energies on other people all week in the work arena. The attitude of "I gave at the office" would be simple to cultivate, especially when working folks are fatigued and could easily grab the first excuse to stay home. But for people like the Hamms, this doesn't seem to be the case. Perhaps because people in a two-paycheck family are especially cognizant that they possess two sets of talents and abilities instead of just one, perhaps because their work environment affirms both the husband's and wife's "gifts" as special and useful, many seem to be imbued with a double dose of commitment to attend worship so they can "give something back to God." The two-paycheck couple's cup often overfloweth—twice—and the knowledge of that sometimes provides the extra push to catapult them out of bed and into a church pew on Sunday mornings.

## For Support From Others

The spacious living room in Mark and Mary Frances Henry's seacoast home, although not opulent, reminded us of the inviting parlour in the movie, *The Great Gatsby*. And the Henrys unabashedly admitted that they had their home designed to create just that type of atmosphere. They wanted it to be a place where people felt free to gather, to circulate, to be themselves. Even the way the furniture was arranged, with sofas and pillows in little clusters, had a master plan behind it: the Henrys are people-lovers, and their home is always open to people in need, to folks who want to talk.

The Henrys are partners in a business called Growthlines. They are consultants in family, interpersonal, and business relationships for industry and non-profit groups. But their sideline involvement is leading intergenerational sessions—small, intimate groups of people of all ages that gather on a biweekly basis to talk about their needs, problems, victories, and joys.

With this as background we were not surprised by Mary Frances's answer to the question of why she makes the effort to attend church after being swamped all week with work: "Seeing the people who have been extremely supportive of me is as vital to me as is the actual worship service itself. You can't live out the Christian faith unless you have contact with others."

Many people find church to be a place where Christ's comforting call in Matthew 11:28, "Come unto me, all ye that labor and are heavy laden, and I will give you rest" (KJV) is carried out. For them, the church is the place where they can find support from the people who know them best and are willing to accept them, "warts and all." Often people who have experienced the love, care, and support of church friends after losing a loved one have been heard to say, "I just wonder what it's like for people who experience a death in the family and don't have church people around to care for them."

Robert Ketchand, who is a member of a two-paycheck family, recently left our community to take a new job at a Washington, D.C., law firm. He made this remark at a church farewell party in his honor: "I have been amazed at the difference in the quality of farewells that we have received in the secular community, as opposed to those in the church community." At work, Robert said, people's comments revolved around his professional value to the law firm and were all couched in language about his productivity, his "keen legal mind." But at church, friends focused on his personal worth, his character, and his spirit. "At work, I had hardly turned in my resignation until they were scrapping over who gets my office furniture," he said. "But at church, they really took some time to mourn our departure."

## To "Be Still and Know"

Unlike most couples we interviewed, Vicki and Mike Black were still skeptical whether the two-paycheck lifestyle would work for their family. Vicki recently went to work as a receptionist in a doctor's office after a fifteen-year absence from the payroll, while she stayed home full time with their daughters, ages thirteen and eight. Her reason for the return was clear: to make ends meet financially for the family. For the Blacks, who are members of a Church of Christ, evenings were still a mad hassle to get supper and to master a few chores before bedtime. And, in Vicki's words, "weekends are a disaster. We just haven't got this whole thing down pat, yet."

It's no wonder then that, when asked why she attends church, Vicki answered, "I enjoy the peace and quiet inside a church building. At church, I have some peace because I'm not having to clean the house or worry about anything."

Bob Lobaugh, technical sales representative for an engineering company, and a Baptist, expressed a similar line of thinking in this way: "At church, our focus is on God and not on problems. If we've had a disagreement, we put it aside for Sunday morning. We start with a central purpose."

Obviously, this type of focusing is part of God's plan for humanity. The Psalmist mentions it when he writes: "Be still, and know that I am God" (Ps. 46:10). In Colossians 3:2 is another reminder: "Set your minds on things that are above, not on things that are on earth." And in Exodus 20:8 we read, "Remember the sabbath day, to keep it holy. Six days you shall labor, and do all your work; but the seventh day is a sabbath to the Lord your God."

Henry Wadsworth Longfellow wrote, "Sunday is the golden clasp that binds together the volume of the week."[3] Many two-paycheck families would say the "binding together" for them comes through church attendance.

## To Cope with Life

It would be hard to find any working couple more active in their church than are Donna and Bob Porter. Donna teaches seventh-grade science at a junior high and Bob is an accountant with a mortgage company; they are parents of a toddler. But they both hold down a number of positions at their small Free Methodist Church and are at church at least three times a week, if not more.

"We go to church on Sunday so we can make it through the rest of the week," says Bob, who is church treasurer, Sunday school secretary, and on the board of trustees and finance committee at the church, which averages between thirty and forty people attending on Sundays.

"On Saturday night, the two of us have a prayer together and pray that the minister will say something we need to hear," says Donna. "Inevitably, that happens the next day."

"The church experience gives you the strength to face everything that comes," says Bob. He also says he believes he would be handicapped in his job if he didn't attend church on Sundays: "The main thing is that it keeps work from getting the best of me. Some of the supervisors there explode about everything. I try to never let this happen to me. People say, 'I don't know how you can remain so calm.' I truly believe that it's because I've been to church that I can keep a cool head."

The Porters' answer was one we expected to hear from virtually every two-paycheck couple we interviewed, although surprisingly we were well into our research before we received that response. But those couples who did echo the Porters' comment shared some very concrete ways they thought being at church translated into their work experience the following week.

Janet Zaozirny, a Lutheran, has a job that few people would envy. As a clinical specialist in psychiatry/mental health, she works with cancer patients at a hospital. "I simply couldn't talk to them and their families if I didn't have some strong religious beliefs, which are taught through the church," she said.

Sandra Lengefeld believes her job as an eighth-grade English teacher gives her an entree to "do a little preaching," in an unobtrusive way, to young people at a critical time in their lives. "If I weren't a Christian and didn't attend church, I might not try to reach those kids," she says.

Her shift-worker husband, Curtis, said his church experience helps him in "conversations with other guys," many of whom live very rough, physical lifestyles: "I don't think I'd try in the least to understand them if it weren't for my religious faith." He says going to church on Sundays keeps him reminded that Christ didn't just stick with the religious crowd but ventured out among the masses and interacted with them in caring ways, whether they were close friends with him or not.

Attending her Catholic church on Sundays helps Beverly Hebert, who works in public relations, keep her job in perspective. She says, "It helps me see my job as simply one part of my life, and that makes frustrations and competitions easier to take in stride."

Although still not sure they can manage the two-paycheck family lifestyle, Vicki and Mike Black have both discovered how the weekly regimen of church helps them survive in the marketplace.

"I work in an office with two other people," says Vicki. "There's always the chance to gossip and backbite. I pray a lot that I'll control my tongue and will try to discourage the other people from using theirs to gossip."

Being a two-paycheck family was a new wrinkle in the lives of Royce and Skip Smith on the day we interviewed them. Royce had gone to work as a school truant officer only two months before. Her husband Skip, supervisor of purchasing at an oil company, had until recently been the sole support of Royce and their two young daughters. Then inflation had forced Royce to join the ranks of the employed.

The Smiths, who are Baptist, made one stipulation when they became a working couple: the new lifestyle absolutely must not interfere with their church activities, because "we've put God at the head of our household," said Skip.

They likely would agree with the Porters, who say church on Sunday helps them get through the week, but would carry it one step further: for them, church on Wednesday night, which they usually attend without fail, is crucial, too. "We can have a rough week, then go on Wednesday night, and that gets us through Thursday and Friday," said Skip.

What would be missing from their work situation if they didn't attend?

"I wouldn't have patience," Royce said. "Ninety-five percent of the people I deal with in truancy situations are lost. But I realize that the way I see these people must be the way God sees me."

Skip said he has a private devotional time while on his

twenty-five-minute commute to work. "I just ask the Lord to use me as his instrument that day. Then I feel much freer to do my job normally."

For many two-paycheck couples, church provides a systematic refresher course on the way God wants his children to live and to relate to others. Without making that weekly effort, the people we interviewed seemed to feel they would more rapidly lose sight of God's standards of conduct. They felt it would be easier for them to slip into behavior patterns which would make them indistinguishable from non-Christians. Perhaps that's why, repeatedly in our interviews, we heard the expression, "I just feel better when I go to church, and I feel lousy during the week if I don't go." Church can be like a shot of adrenalin that energizes a working couple for the week's tasks.

## A Special Reason for Two-Paycheck Couples

To all these valid reasons, Kay and I offer our own beliefs for why church is a must for a two-paycheck family. Even in the traditional marriage, with only one spouse working outside the home, there is a monumental amount of tension generated by work-related problems. Cranky bosses, rude customers, ethical decisions, even the press of daily rush-hour traffic can make a work week unbearable for the spouse who is employed. The family desperately needs a place to go at week's end for a refueling—for a brush-up session on how God expects a Christian to conduct his business.

But in a two-paycheck family, the situation is compounded. Here, there are two people involved—each with his or her own interoffice politics to master. Both husband and wife have to deal with their respective hostile publics during the week. Each has to answer to a boss; each has to make decisions of right and wrong about a particular set of problems. Then they come home, and whereas the spouse in the single-paycheck family can often find a sympathetic ear to unload his problems on in the evening, members of a two-paycheck family often find themselves locking horns over who had the worst day.

In the two-paycheck family, then, church becomes almost obligatory. Here, two weary pilgrims can find solace and refurbishment for the week ahead. Although church preparation can cause a certain amount of tension, church itself can be a safety valve that can actually relieve some of the stress in a two-paycheck marriage. If only one sentence in a minister's message hits home and relates to that person in his work pilgrimage, it may keep the other spouse from having to be the "be-all, end-all" to that person when she is burdened with her own work-related woes.

Like many couples, Kay and I often can sit through the same thirty-minute sermon and come home insisting we caught two separate points from it. But if each of those points helps us individually in some way in our week ahead, it matters little that we don't agree on the overriding theme. Because in many ways two-paycheck families have "double trouble," they also need "double strength" to cope. Like many of the couples we interviewed, we believe that regular church experience can be a powerful "double strength" tablet.

# 3. Some Biblical Dimensions

I could hardly wait to get Pastor Jones on the telephone. In searching for two-paycheck families to interview for our book, we often contacted pastors such as Jones to get the names of active members of their churches whom they felt coped well with the two-paycheck lifestyle. I had zeroed in on this pastor because he was known in his community for his theologically "liberal" stance on a variety of matters. He was affiliated with the United Presbyterian Church, U.S.A., a denomination noted for its stand on the equality of women. I assumed he would quickly spiel off the names of several working couples among his membership, and Kay and I would be in business to start our interviews.

I couldn't have been more shocked at his answer to our request. He was quiet a long time, muttering, "I'm thinking. I'm thinking . . ." Finally, he blurted out, "I just can't think of a single two-paycheck couple in this entire church." Furthermore, he seemed to have some trouble even understanding why two-paycheck families in the church could possibly be an appropriate subject for a book.

Just the converse was true in the case of Pastor Smith. I had dallied around for days before contacting this minister, because he was pastor of a Southern Baptist church and was noted for his heavy fundamentalist leanings. Every time I picked up the phone to call this minister to get the names

of two-paycheck couples in his congregation, I would put
it down, telling myself that I just wasn't ready to listen
to what I was sure would be a sermon on "why women
should stay home where they belong."

Finally, I bit the bullet and contacted him. Again, as with
Pastor Jones, I couldn't have been more surprised—but for
an entirely different reason. Instead of the lecture I expected,
this pastor tuned in immediately with our project.

"Why, that's an excellent idea," he said. "I know lots
of couples in our church just like the people you are seeking.
I am sure there's really a need for a book like yours." He
then rattled off a long list of names of working couples—
far too many for us to use from any one church.

What a reversal! The theological liberal couldn't tune in
with our project, but the fundamentalist almost bowled
me over with his enthusiasm. And I had thought just the
opposite would occur. After we completed our interviews
and research, I continued to mull over these two contradic-
tory conversations.

Finally I realized that there was another highly significant
factor involved besides the theological leanings of the ministers. The Presbyterian church was situated in an affluent
section in its community, near neighborhoods populated
by prosperous bankers and oil company executives. The
Baptist church, on the other hand, was situated in an eco-
nomically and socially changing neighborhood. In the
wealthy sector where the Presbyterian church had its ministry, the right of women to work outside the home was
more of a philosophical idea. In the Baptist church's neighborhood, two paychecks were an economic necessity for
many families.

These two phone calls also shed some new light on the
way church friends had behaved when Kay first returned
to her newspaper job after our son was born. We had been
members of a conservative Baptist church which was not
far removed theologically from the fundamentalist church
whose pastor eagerly helped with our book project. But it

was located in the same type of neighborhood as the Presbyterian church whose pastor could barely tune into our subject matter. Suddenly we could see why Baptist residents of this affluent neighborhood had responded in the same way as did the reluctant Presbyterian pastor.

The two-paycheck issue is often presented as a theological one. The women in our Sunday school class who prayed that Barbara would not follow Kay's example of returning to work after her child was born did so, they thought, for theological reasons. They believed it was God's will for a mother to stay home and tend to her husband, children, and house. But, as our experience with the Presbyterian and Baptist ministers taught us, the issue often transcends theological lines. It often has as much to do with the culture in which people live as with their theological bias.

## Cultural Attitudes Vary, Too

Before we go further, I think it is important that we reflect on how cultural attitudes toward two-paycheck families have varied during past centuries. The concept of working couples is not a new idea developed in the 1980s. Centuries ago the Industrial Revolution brought women out of their homes and into the marketplace to work alongside their husbands in business and industry. In nineteenth-century England, for instance, the two-paycheck marriage was a matter of class: having a wife at home instead of in the factory was a luxury Englishmen of the poorer classes could not afford.

Too, no one today can accurately compare the lifestyle of farm couples during the last century or early in this century with the "husband at work, wife at home" model emphasized today. The farmer and his wife were much more akin to the working couples of today than to the housewife who "stays home" in the suburbs while her husband goes off to earn the family's living in the city.

The modern notion that the wife belongs at home all

day with the children while the husband goes off to work to provide an income is largely a product of the post-war 1950s. During World War II, wives made the bombs and the airplanes and staffed the plants and watched the home-front while their husbands went to fight in the war. "Rosie the Riveter" became a national symbol of women at work in wartime. When the GIs returned home, they wanted to repay their wives by retiring them to the luxury of new homes equipped with the latest in modern conveniences.

In that box of old pictures and memorabilia my mother recently gave me was a letter my father wrote to my mother from the Pacific, where he fought in Gen. Douglas MacArthur's gallant effort to regain the Philippines and other territories seized by the Japanese during World War II. In the letter, Dad pledges to Mom that when the war is over he will come home and get a job, that she will never have to work again. My father, I believe, was expressing an attitude that prevailed among many servicemen during World War II. Those men looked forward to a postwar prosperity that would enable their wives to give up their war-enforced duties and stay home with the "baby boom" babies of the late 1940s and early 1950s. In the 1950s, the men went off to the offices or factories to get ahead, often leaving their wives with small children and with a new life that was much easier than earlier generations had known.

It is against this cultural background as much as any biblical teachings that today's struggle between those who believe a wife shouldn't work and those who think a woman has a right to be in the marketplace must be understood.

## Economic Necessity or Personal Fulfillment?

Another experience just after Kay returned to work served to affirm this dichotomy of culture and Bible for us. About the same time Kay went back to her newspaper job, another young woman in our Sunday school class put her small child in a day-care center and took a clerical job.

Unlike Kay, however, this woman, named Jan, made it clear to one and all that she was working strictly for economic necessity. Career goals had nothing to do with her decision. She and her husband needed the money, and her going to work was the only answer for them.

Curiously, Jan said she never felt the same type of criticism from other church members Kay had felt, even though her circle of friends was basically the same as ours. In fact, we recall that Jan experienced only sympathy and even pity from other members of her Sunday school class. For several weeks during that time, no one referred to Jan without calling her "Poor Jan"—"poor" almost becoming a part of her name. If the group that criticized Kay had attacked Jan for working, Jan probably would have chimed right in with their criticism. She preferred to be at home, but could not financially afford to be. So she took the only route open to her.

For members of this affluent church we attended, economic need seemed to be the only "valid" reason for a two-paycheck family. Although Kay's course of action was no different than Jan's, somehow the women in the Sunday school class implied that God looked less kindly on us because Kay returned to work for reasons of self-fulfillment rather than financial need. It was as though Jan became the "good working mother" because of her motivations, while Kay was pegged as the "bad working mother." Therefore, Jan did not hear implications about God's will, but Kay did.

Kay and I realize that this story of Jan reflects the broader issue of hypocrisy in churches, but it also shows how theological issues are used—not always consistently—against the two-paycheck family.

We were not the only couple who encountered opposition to their lifestyle based on theological grounds. And, as in the cases we cited, the opposition did not necessarily occur along denominational lines.

## Bracing for Theological Battles

I called long distance to set up a personal interview with Rita and Jack Newton. But the moment I explained our project, Rita began pouring out her troubles over the telephone lines. She had been an elementary school teacher before their child was born, and she wanted to return to work as soon as the child was in grade school. In the meantime, she wanted to enroll in graduate study.

But Rita was spooked by some hair-raising tales she had been told about what had happened when other mothers in the Church of Christ congregation she attended resumed their jobs.

According to Rita, women in their California congregation who returned to work with children at home were visited by elders of the congregation and were instructed not to continue working. In one case, the elders even visited the babysitter of a woman who had just taken a job, telling the sitter she was doing wrong by keeping the children of women who work. The elders claimed the church teaches that a woman who sits with the children of other women who work outside the home becomes something akin to an accomplice to a crime.

Just before I called, Rita had stopped attending the church's ladies' Bible class because of her teacher's statements about the role of women. The teacher, wife of one of the church's elders, went to visit Rita after the two had had a disagreement in the class. "She [the teacher] left in a state of shock at what I said," said Rita. "I disagreed with several things she mentioned about the role of women, and I told her so. She said it was a pity that I didn't realize how great motherhood is and what a woman's role should be in the world."

Rita said a woman at her church who is a working wife and mother was offered a management position in her company. A few days after news about the promotion got out, two women from the congregation arrived to tell the friend that she should refuse the job. They claimed the Bible teaches that women should not be in a supervisory position over men.

Rita refused to return to the ladies' Bible class at her church. At last report, she and Jack were frantically reading the New Testament, especially the letters of Paul, to better equip themselves to answer criticism and to counter arguments about working women in the congregation.

Gay McFarland, a writer, says one of the main reasons she stopped attending her Bible church before her marriage to writer John Scarborough was the church's teachings on working wives. The large church she attended taught that the Bible says women belong at home with the children, not in the workaday world.

At the time we interviewed them, John and Gay were "sitting out" church for awhile. Like many other couples, they were not sure how they would handle the churchless situation when children came. But one thing was certain for them: a tolerant attitude about two-paycheck families likely would be their strongest criterion for choosing a church when they do reach a decision. "I'm just not going to belong to a church where I feel I'm a second-class citizen for working," said Gay. "There are too many stresses already associated with working, and the church shouldn't add to them by making women feel bad when they earn a paycheck."

Linda and Eric King, both attorneys and parents of three children, say they have received criticism of their lifestyle at their Church of Christ in Oklahoma. "Many people, including our present preacher, still believe a woman's place is in the home. They view it as a religious matter. Thus, to some extent, a woman is usurping a man's place when she leaves her domestic domain. We have had sermons intimating this, along with paeans to housewives," said Linda.

Since the matter is so often bandied about, let's look at what the Bible truly does say about the two-paycheck family and whether it really teaches that the woman's place is always in the home. But before we look at some key Bible verses on this matter, let's first review our understanding of what role the Bible should play in our lives and how it is to be interpreted.

## Understanding the Bible

The Bible is mankind's record of God's revelation of himself to man. It contains the truth about God. It was written by people whom God guided. We like the way *Christianity Today*, the evangelical fortnightly publication, described this revelation to the biblical writers: "No evangelical scholar defends the idea that God dictated the Bible by a method analogous to the way a businessman dictates a letter to his stenographer. The few who (unwisely, we think) use the term 'dictate' mean only that the end product is just as much the word of God as though the whole Bible had been dictated by God."[1]

The Bible is also our guide for living. It is divine authority. With the help of the Holy Spirit for interpretation, it is the most important book we have to help us understand God. We believe the Bible should be read, studied, and followed.

But we must not make the Bible more than what it claims to be. It is not a scientific textbook. According to that same article in *Christianity Today*, "Inerrancy does not mean that the Bible always uses exact language. It does not require that the Bible employ up-to-date scientific terminology. Evangelicals are not trying to make the Bible into a science textbook; they mean only that it is true."[2]

We also understand that the Bible was written in the context of its culture. No one (at least that we know) believes that, because King David had many wives, men today should be polygamous. By the same token, no one believes that, because Abraham fathered a child by a mistress, men today should be free to pursue such activities. The Bible records the actions of sinful people who lived in various cultures—some that are alien to our present way of Christian living.

We must take care that we do not remove the cultural patterns, which provided the environment for the writing of the Bible, and superimpose them indiscriminately on our culture today.

So how then should we read the Bible? We should approach our study with an attitude of prayer, seeking the wisdom of the Holy Spirit. We do not need any key, such as Mary Baker Eddy's *Science for Living,* or Joseph Smith's *Book of Mormon* to unlock the Scriptures. Modern commentaries can help us understand the background of the Bible. But such commentaries do not take precedent over the Bible.

## Let the Bible Speak to You

There are two ways to read the Bible: (1) to let it speak to you in ways that were intended, or (2) to make it speak to you in ways that you want to hear. Theologians have two fancy words to describe these methods: *exegesis* and *eisegesis.* Exegesis means to understand what the Bible is saying to you. Eisegesis means to read into the Bible things you want it to say. We must be careful that we do not use the Bible to say what we want it to.

In Oklahoma, where I was reared, there was an uneducated Baptist preacher who seemed to fall into the second category. This preacher strongly disliked a popular hairstyle of the day—the topknot, formed by wrapping a woman's long hair into a bun on top of her head. In order to preach against the topknot, this preacher studied the Bible intently, looking for the key verses. He found what he was seeking in Mark 13:15, although he had to adjust his spelling a little. In the verse, Jesus was speaking about turbulent times to come. Jesus said, "Let him that is on the housetop not go down into the house." By adding the letter *k* to the word *not,* and by doing a little surgery on the verse, the pastor had the text of his sermon: "Top (k)not go down." He projected onto the Bible what he wanted to find. We must read the Bible in context to avoid making the same error.

## The Working Couples in the Bible

The central theological question working couples need to answer is this: What does the Bible say about the two-paycheck lifestyle?

Our answer: The Bible is essentially silent on the matter. Working couples were simply not an issue when the Bible was being written. There are, however, two important examples of working couples in the Scriptures—Priscilla and Aquila in the New Testament and the "virtuous wife" in Proverbs.

Acts 18:3 says Priscilla and Aquila, a husband and wife, were both tentmakers. Paul stayed with them in Corinth because, the Scriptures say, "He was of the same trade."

Besides their work with tents, Priscilla and Aquila also worked together as teachers. They were instrumental in the doctrinal education of Apollos. Acts 18:24–26 describes Apollos as "a Jew . . . a native of Alexandria. . . . an eloquent man, well versed in the scriptures. He had been instructed in the way of the Lord; and being fervent in spirit, he spoke and taught accurately the things concerning Jesus, though he knew only the baptism of John." The Scriptures say that Priscilla and Aquila heard Apollos, then "they took him and expounded to him the way of God more accurately."

From the story of Priscilla and Aquila, we know that at least one working husband and wife were actively involved in the early church.

The other example of a working couple is found in the Old Testament. The description of the "virtuous wife" in the thirty-first chapter of Proverbs seems to describe an ideal woman of early Bible days who does the same kind

of balancing act between home, family, and career that
many modern working couples do. According to Proverbs
31:10–18, "Who can find a wife with strength of character?
She is far more precious than jewels. The heart of her husband trusts in her, and he will never lack profit. She does
him good and not harm all the days of her life; she seeks
wool and flax, and works with willing hands; she is like
the merchant ships; she brings her food from afar. She rises
while it is yet night, and gives food to her household, even
a portion to her maidens; she considers a field and buys
it; with the fruit of her hands she plants a vineyard. She
girds her loins with strength, and makes her arms strong.
She sees that her merchandise is profitable; her lamp does
not go out at night" (MLB). Whether the virtuous wife described here was an early real estate person, a produce
grower, or a garment maker who sewed for the public, we
do not know. But it seems clear that she was engaged in
a business of some sort. She also was capable of performing
superior intellectual tasks, and the Scripture does not seem
to view this capability as an indication of masculinity in
a woman.

Except for these two brief examples, there is little direct
biblical reference to two-paycheck couples. Jesus does not
address the issue of working couples directly; neither does
Paul, nor do any other biblical writers. But while the Bible
is essentially silent on the issue of working couples, it does
offer some pertinent teachings on several related companion
issues—the use of God-given talents, the role of women,
Christian marriage, and how Christians are to treat one another.

## The Use of God-Given Talents

Christian vocalist Cynthia Clawson had just returned
from one of her frequent out-of-town engagements when
we met. At home in their living room, she and her husband,
composer and actor Ragan Courtney, who are Baptists, dis-

cussed their hectic and unorthodox lifestyle. Several weeks out of each month, Cynthia travels to various American cities giving vocal concerts. While she is gone from home, Ragan stays home with their toddler son, Will, and writes and composes.

How does Ragan feel about his wife's travels and about her being in the spotlight so often? Ragan's answer was simple and straight from the teachings of Jesus. "The biblical parable of the talents teaches that you do not bury talents," said Ragan. He believes God has given Cynthia talents he wants her to use.[3]

The story of the talents is found in Matthew 25:14–30. Although the word *talent* in the parable actually refers to a coin, the implication is wider, and could also refer to God-given abilities. In the story, Jesus encouraged his followers to use wisely what God has given them. In this parable, the follower who failed to use God's gifts was punished.

Both men and women are given talents by God. Those talents are not limited to what any one culture labels as male or female. Some men have a special knack for cooking. Some women have a talent to manage business affairs. God was no respector of gender when he distributed abilities. The Bible makes it clear what happens when special gifts are allowed to lie dormant—and this admonition was not merely directed at men.

I was especially impressed with Ragan's response about his wife's talents, because I identified heavily with his feeling. I encourage Kay to pursue her writing career because I believe her ability comes from God—that's the way I feel about mine, too. If we did not use our talents, we would be like the servant in Jesus' parable who ran and hid his talent for fear of losing it. When questioned by his master, that servant replied, "Master, I knew you to be a hard man, reaping where you did not sow, and gathering where you did not winnow; so I was afraid, and I went and hid your talent in the ground" (Matt. 25:24–25).

Then the master said to him: "You wicked and slothful servant! You knew that I reap where I have not sowed, and gather where I have not winnowed? Then you ought to have invested my money with the bankers, and at my coming I should have received what was my own with interest" (vv. 26–27). Then the master took the servant's talent from him and gave it to another, casting "the worthless servant into the outer darkness" (v. 30).

## Working Women in the Bible

Another companion issue to that of working couples is the issue of working women. A couple today usually becomes a two-paycheck family when the wife joins her husband as a breadwinner. The idea of working men is neither new nor controversial; it is the idea of working women that generates controversy in some quarters today. It is not our purpose here to argue the whole feminist issue of equal pay, equal opportunities, or equal rights. We are specifically interested in what the Bible says about women—especially wives—working outside the home.

We recognize that many of the women in the Bible were homemakers and not business women. But contrary to popular misconception, there are a number of career women mentioned in both the Old and New Testaments.

Deborah is described in Judges 4:4 as a "prophetess." She was the wife of Lapidoth. She also was a judge of Israel, which means she was the ranking Jewish leader of her time. We could call her the Golda Meir of the Israel of her day. Judges 4:5 says Deborah sat on a hill under a palm "and the people of Israel came up to her for judgment."

Deborah became a great military leader when the leading Hebrew officer, Barak, refused to go into battle without her at his side. According to Judges 4:8–9, Barak said to Deborah, "If you will go with me, I will go; but if you will not go with me, I will not go." And Deborah said to Barak, "I will surely go with you; nevertheless, the road on which you are going will not lead to your glory, for the Lord will sell Sisera into the hand of a woman." Of course Deborah won the battle and gained fame as a leader in battle.

One of Paul's first converts was a working woman, Lydia, from the city of Thyatira. Paul met her while meeting with some women who had gathered for prayer "outside the gate to the riverside" of Philippi, the leading city of the district of Macedonia. The story of that encounter is told in Acts 16:11–15.

Lydia is identified in the Scriptures as a "seller of purple," which is generally interpreted as meaning purple cloth. Although the Bible does not state whether she was married, it seems clear that Lydia was a prosperous business woman, because she maintained a household and had her own home. Acts 16:15 says, "And when she [Lydia] was baptized, with her household, she besought us, saying, 'If you have judged me to be faithful to the Lord, come to my house and stay.' And she prevailed upon us."

Paul must have been impressed with Lydia, for he returned to her home after being locked up in the Macedonian jail. Acts 16:40 reports, "So they went out of the prison, and visited Lydia; and when they had seen the brethren, they exhorted them and departed."

Phoebe was another leading woman of the New Testament. We do not know what career she pursued, but we know that she played a key role in the early church and had duties beyond that of homemaker. Several scholars believe Paul entrusted his letter to the Romans to Phoebe for delivery. Austin H. Stouffer, in a *Christianity Today* article on the ordination of women, calls it a "task many of our churches would delegate only to men."[4] Stouffer and others also point out that Phoebe was a deaconess in the early church, possibly the only female deacon in the church. In Romans 16:1–2, Paul said, "I commend to you our sister Phoebe, a deaconess of the church at Cenchreae, that you may receive her in the Lord as befits the saints, and help

her in whatever she may require from you, for she has
been a helper of many and of myself as well."

## What Did Jesus and Paul
## Say about Working Women?

Any biblical discussion about working women must include a discussion about what Jesus and Paul said and taught
about women working outside the home.

Jesus never said that a woman's place is in the home.
Nor did he say a woman's place is in the marketplace. He
did not speak directly to the question of two-paycheck marriage. But Jesus did say much in both words and deeds
about the value and worth of persons, male and female.
It is from these teachings that we must draw our understanding of what he might say today about working women.

Many writers and theologians have pointed out that Jesus'
attitude toward women stood in sharp contrast to the customs of his day. A clear example of this is John 4:7–42,
in which Jesus tells the woman at the well in Samaria that
she had five former husbands and a current live-in boyfriend. For two reasons, the woman was shocked that Jesus
would speak to her: (1) she was a Samaritan, and Jews
had no dealings with these people, who were actually their
relatives; and (2) she was a woman, perhaps of ill repute.
Jesus treated this woman of Samaria with respect, understanding, and forgiveness. Her testimony later served to
tell the people of her village about Jesus. Jesus knew and
respected the worth of this woman and violated traditional
customs in winning her admiration forever.

The Mary, Martha, and Lazarus story in the New Testament also gives us a clue as to Jesus' attitudes where women
were concerned. As Jesus went to visit this brother and
two sisters who lived in Bethany near Jerusalem, Martha
became so busy preparing the meal for her houseguest that
she could not listen to all that Jesus had to say. Mary listened
intently. Finally Martha asked Jesus to tell Mary to leave

his side and to help her with meal preparations. Jesus scolded Martha, telling her that there were values greater than a well-prepared meal and a spotless dish. Here, Jesus had the perfect chance to lecture Mary on the role of women, telling her to stay at home and tend to the culinary and domestic arts. Instead, he told Martha that she too should be listening, using her God-given thinking and reasoning abilities.

In Luke 8:1–3, we learn that women as well as men were instrumental in Jesus' ministry. "After this he [Jesus] went journeying from town to town and village to village, proclaiming the good news of the kingdom of God. With him were the Twelve and a number of women who had been set free from evil spirits and infirmities: Mary, known as Mary of Magdala, from whom seven devils had come out, Joanna, the wife of Chuza a steward of Herod's, Susanna, and many others. These women provided for them out of their own resources" (NEB). The use of the term, "own resources" indicates that the women did more than just to offer their talents and physical labor. They offered funds. Apparently, these were women of some means who shared their financial resources with Jesus and his disciples.

Later, at the time of Jesus' death, some of these women were standing near the cross. In Luke 23:49, we learn that, "His [Jesus'] friends had all been standing at a distance [watching the crucifixion]; the women who had accompanied him from Galilee stood with them and watched it all" (NEB). Then, after Jesus' body was removed from the cross, these women were the ones who "followed . . . took note of the tomb and observed how his body was laid. Then they went home and prepared spices and perfumes" (NEB). Two days later, on that first Easter morning, these were the women who reported the resurrection. So their role in the conclusion of Jesus' earthly ministry was crucial.

Could it be that some of the first bearers of the Good News of the resurrection were businesswomen? We don't know for sure. The Scriptures only tell us about Joanna's husband's job. The idea that Mary Magdala was a reformed prostitute is merely conjecture. We don't know whether she had a husband or how she supported herself. We also don't know any of these details about Susanna and the "many other" women who traveled with Jesus. The fact that these women traversed the country freely with Jesus and his disciples and had their own money to underwrite the journeys indicate that these were not typical homemakers of Jesus' day.

It's interesting to speculate that these were business women, or maybe partners in some two-paycheck lifestyle. We won't commit the same error the Oklahoma preacher did and try to read too much into Bible verses. But one thing is certain: Jesus did not encourage these women to hide their abilities and intelligence, and he associated with them freely.

Paul was the bridge between Jews and Gentiles in spreading the gospel; it was he who took the life, death, and resurrection of Jesus and interpreted them to the world outside of Judaism. Paul was "the man most responsible for carrying the Christian faith to the Graeco-Roman world beyond Palestine," says one source book. "Beginning his career as a fierce persecutor of the earliest followers of Jesus, he experienced a miraculous conversion, and from that time on he practiced Christian evangelism so zealously and successfully that he went down in history as the revered 'apostle to the Gentiles.' "[5]

An entire book could be written on Paul's views on women. In fact, Paul's is the name that usually comes up when the discussion turns to women's roles. In an editorial on "Women's Role in Church and Family," *Christianity Today* says, "The role of women in the home is more difficult to determine because of the interlacing of scripture and cultural patterns both in ancient and modern times." Every example used in the editorial after that statement came from the writings of Paul.[6]

We have neither the time nor the space to go into every

detail of what Paul said about the role of women. We want, therefore, to concentrate on Paul's attitude toward women working outside the home.

Paul is like Jesus on the issue of working women. He never said a woman's place is always at home, nor did he say that a woman's place is never in the marketplace. Some people read certain passages from Paul and conclude that he was opposed to working women. We believe these are only interpretations of people who set out to prove a certain premise.

When Royce Smith was preparing to take her job as truant officer, she and husband Skip, a purchasing supervisor, decided to enroll in a seminar on financial management offered at a neighborhood Baptist church.

To Royce's shock, the Baptist pastor who taught the course kicked off the opening night talk by attempting to "prove," using two verses from Paul, that women should not work outside the home. Part of his text was 1 Timothy 5:8: "If any one does not provide for his relatives . . . he has disowned the faith and is worse than an unbeliever." The other part of the minister's text was Titus 2:3–5: "Bid the older women likewise to be reverent in behavior, not to be slanderers or slaves to drink; they are to teach what is good, and so train the young women to love their husbands and children, to be sensible, chaste, domestic, kind, and submissive to their husbands, that the word of God may not be discredited."

Royce said the pastor's words at first made her apprehensive: "I felt like my decision [to go back to work] had been God's will. My first reaction was, 'Maybe I didn't pray hard enough.' So I prayed again and got the same answer—that this was the right step for me."

The two verses from Paul quoted by the pastor at the financial seminar in no way exclude women from working outside the home. We believe it is possible for modern women to use their talents outside the home and still meet all the requirements of the two verses: loving their hus-

bands, caring for children, and being sensible, chaste, domestic, kind, and yes, even submissive—a term that gets
tossed around a lot in discussions about working women.
We'll pick up on the subject of submission in a few pages
when we explore the meaning of Christian marriage.

Back to Paul's specific comments about working women:
We have already cited two passages that indicate Paul had
golden opportunities to lecture working women about their
lifestyle—the cases of Lydia and Priscilla. But there is no
indication in the passages concerning Paul's relationship
with Lydia which would indicate that he frowned upon
her career. In fact, it could be argued that he willingly accepted the hospitality which her income and status allowed
her to offer him. Lydia is, moreover, immortalized in the
scriptures as "the seller of purple," just as professional
women today want to be remembered as journalists, doctors, lawyers, real estate brokers and so on.

In his relationship with Priscilla and Aquila, Paul had
the perfect opportunity to lecture or scold Priscilla about
working alongside her husband in the tentmaking business.
Paul never seemed to hesitate expressing his disapproval
of other customs or behavior he considered wrong. Yet there
is no indication whatsoever that Paul disapproved of this
two-paycheck marriage.

In both cases, we believe Paul's silence on the issue of
working women is significant.

Several other women played key roles in the life and
ministry of Paul. We do not know whether all these women
pursued careers outside the home. But we do know that
women were not excluded from a vital role in the early
church. Said Austin H. Stouffer in his article on the ordination of women, "Of the twenty-nine people Paul greets
in Romans 16, many are women he addressed by name,
contrary to Jewish custom: Phoebe, Tryphaena, Tryphosa,
Julia, Mary."[7]

Though Paul is often placed in the role of an opponent
to modern working women, we feel that image is un-
founded. Our study of Scripture does not show Paul to

be opposed to women being in the marketplace, as some would have us believe.

## What the Bible Says about Marriage

Another biblical issue that relates to the two-paycheck family is that of Christian marriage.

It is important to reflect on two passages from Genesis in the Old Testament which set forth the principles on which Christian marriage is based. In the Genesis creation story, we find: "So God created man in his own image, in the image of God he created him; male and female he created them. And God blessed them. . . ." (Gen. 1:27–28). Then, a few verses further, we find the second creation story of man and woman, in Genesis 2:7, 21–24: "Then the Lord God formed man of dust from the ground, and breathed into his nostrils the breath of life; and man became a living being. . . . So the Lord God caused a deep sleep to fall upon the man, and while he slept took one of his ribs and closed up its place with flesh; and the rib which the Lord God had taken from the man he made into a woman and brought her to the man. Then the man said, 'This at last is bone of my bones and flesh of my flesh; she shall be called Woman, because she was taken out of Man.' Therefore a man leaves his father and his mother and cleaves to his wife, and they become one flesh."

In these beautiful verses, which tell us of the first marriage and the first couple, we see that God created each of us— male and female—in his image. That means we each have value and worth, regardless of whether we are male or female. Many people have pointed out that God did not choose to remove a portion of Adam's foot to make Eve, to show that woman is beneath man. Nor did he remove a portion of Adam's head, to show that woman is above man. God instead chose to remove a portion of Adam's rib to show that woman stands beside man. Man and woman are to be together, side by side.

It is this side-by-side partnership that we feel is essential for a two-paycheck marriage—and any marriage—to work. In a successful two-paycheck lifestyle, husbands and wives must see themselves as involved in a partnership where both persons benefit from the relationship and the marriage, just as Adam and Eve benefited from each other. A couple must work together—side by side—to make the lifestyle work.

## Understanding Submission

Now, back to the verses from Paul on submission. These verses continually pop up like a jack-in-the-box as the theological basis for opposition to women working outside the home. The key verses on this subject are found in Ephesians 5. To understand Paul's teachings on the roles of husbands and wives, it is absolutely essential that we read these verses in context and in their entirety.

Paul wrote, "Wives, be subject to your husbands, as to the Lord. For the husband is the head of the wife as Christ is the head of the church, his body, and himself its Savior. As the church is subject to Christ, so let wives also be subject in everything to their husbands." At this point, many opponents of the two-paycheck lifestyle stop reading their Bibles and start preaching. But Paul's thoughts do not stop here. They continue on: "Husbands, love your wives, as Christ loved the church and gave himself up for her, that he might sanctify her, having cleansed her by the washing of water with the word, that he might present the church to himself in splendor, without spot or wrinkle or any such thing, that she might be holy and without blemish. Even so husbands should love their wives as their own bodies. He who loves his wife loves himself. For no man ever hates his own flesh, but nourishes and cherishes it, as Christ does the church, because we are members of his body. 'For this reason a man shall leave his father and mother and be joined to his wife, and the two shall become one flesh.' This mystery is a profound one, and I am saying that it refers to Christ and the church; however, let each one of you love his wife as himself, and let the wife see that she respects her husband" (Eph. 5:25–33).

In these verses, Paul was talking about the spiritual organization of the family. He spoke about a mutual relationship between a husband and wife, in which both are treated with respect, appreciation, and love. Paul was not advocating a tyranny where a husband walks all over his wife. He told a wife to respect her husband and his place in the family, and he told a husband to respect his wife and treat her with love.

We concur with Paul in saying that any major decision in a family must be made jointly and with love and with respect. It is essential that the decision to become a two-paycheck family be made in an environment in which the husband loves his wife enough that he wants what is best for her.

The husband must love his wife enough to want her to be fulfilled as a person and to view her role as important. If working will help her find that fulfillment, then a husband should understand and work with his wife in order to achieve that goal. And the wife should love her husband and respect him enough to understand his wishes on the subject and to seek his counsel about the venture before she makes the decision.

Paul was correct: There are two people, two opinions, two sets of standards and feelings to take into account in every marriage. We say "amen" to Paul's statement, "Let each one of you love his wife as himself and let the wife see that she respects her husband." To us, it seems to affirm, not contradict, the basic premise of the two-paycheck marriage.

## How Christians Are to Treat One Another

There is a fourth companion issue to any discussion about two-paycheck families in the church. As we have shown, the Bible never directly addresses the issue of working couples. But it is clear as a bell about the way Christians are to treat one another—even those who disagree with them. The biblical standard for relating to others is love, patience, and a nonjudgmental attitude. This applies both to the churches and the two-paycheck families.

"Judge not, that ye be not judged. For with what judgment ye judge, ye shall be judged," said Jesus (Matt. 7:1, KJV). At another point, Jesus said, "Love thy neighbor as thyself" (Mark 12:31, KJV). Those are verses which much always be recalled when Christians are discussing issues on which there is disagreement.

Churches as well as one-paycheck families have an obligation to refrain from making cruel and unnecessary judgments about two-paycheck families. And two-paycheck families have an equal obligation to seek to understand and love those who disagree with their style of living. We'll write more about this later in the chapter on how to handle criticism.

## An Issue Each Couple Must Decide

We believe, in view of the Bible's essential silence on this issue, that becoming a two-paycheck family is a matter each couple must decide for themselves. Before joining the growing number of working couples, each couple must answer three questions to their own satisfaction:

(1) *What is God through the Bible saying to us about becoming a two-paycheck family?* It is best to follow Royce and Skip Smith's pattern and turn to God for advice and counsel, rather than relying on current fads or off-the-cuff decisions.

(2) *Do we agree together on what we should do?* Both partners in the marriage should agree on the lifestyle they will pursue. They need to work together as a team, whether they become a two-paycheck family or choose to remain a one-paycheck family.

(3) *Can we handle the demands of a two-paycheck marriage without*

*endangering ourselves spiritually?* Remember: nothing is more important than one's relationship to God—not even the husband's nor the wife's employment. The advice our minister gave us when we married is very appropriate here: your first loyalty is to God; your second is to each other; your third is to any children born to the union; and your fourth is to your careers. We would urge all couples to let their faith be the guiding force in all decisions—including the decision whether or not to become a two-paycheck family.

# 4. Putting First Things First

Jane's husband is pastor of a new, fast-growing Baptist church in a small city. She's never worked outside the home except for a few brief weeks of being a substitute teacher in a nearby high school—a job which she described as "physically draining and impossible." Her husband hardly knows a dish towel from a bath towel. Without her, he'd be lost if he ever had to perform such a simple household chore as sorting the clothes for the laundry.

Yet this full-time homemaker understands a principle that every two-paycheck couple must learn when trying to put together two careers, a strong marriage, children, and the church. She's learned how to set priorities in her church schedule.

Although on the surface it seems that Jane, as part of a one-paycheck family, might have far more time to carry a heavy load at church than would a member of a two-paycheck marriage, she has consistently refused to take on more church jobs than she knew she could handle.

Even when their congregation was just beginning and there were few available bodies to work, Jane stood firm on refusing to become an unpaid staff member—the trap that many pastors' wives fall into. Instead, she lives by this credo: "I zero in on one thing to do at church, and do it well."

Jane's "bag" is directing the Sunday school department for fourth, fifth, and sixth graders. Watching her conduct this department is like watching a maestro conduct a symphony orchestra. On Sunday mornings, she enters the front door with several boxes of materials and visual aids that she has prepared for that week's lessons. During the week, she telephones every youngster who has been absent the previous Sunday, to express her love and interest in him. During the Bible-study hour, the usually fidgety youngsters listen with rapt attention to her appealing presentation. At Sunday school teaching, it's obvious that Jane is a real pro.

But this one teaching assignment is the only job that Jane undertakes at church. She doesn't belong to any committees. She doesn't sing in the choir. She attends worship regularly, but she is not the motivating force behind the women's group, nor is she the primary typist in the church office. Even though her husband is a regular speaker at church groups throughout the week, Jane seldom attends these meetings.

"I would rather select one job and do it first-class than to spread myself too thin in lots of areas," she says. Jane has boldly rejected the idea that she should be the "assistant to the pastor" or the leading lay woman in the congregation.

If setting boundaries and establishing priorities on church activities are important to this homemaker/minister's wife, just think how much more vital they are to the two-paycheck couple! When both husband and wife work, time is extremely crucial, and scheduling must be handled with as much care as is the family's budget. "If you have a lot of money, you don't have to budget quite as tightly," says marriage and family counselor Lavonia Duck, a Baptist. "The same thing applies to time. If you have a lot of it, you don't have to be quite so selective."

Many of the couples we interviewed talked openly about the tight schedule on which they must operate, and not one disagreed with our assumption that time is a valuable commodity in a two-paycheck family. One couple, in fact, insisted that they could allot us no more than forty-five minutes of their time for our interview. That couple was polite but firm about keeping us to our time commitment. To spare any more obviously would have disrupted carefully outlined plans for their Sunday afternoon.

In thinking about choosing church activities for a two-paycheck family with a tight schedule, we have found the image of a cafeteria line to be helpful. Like a cafeteria where many tempting varieties of food are served, the church usually offers more programs than the average two-paycheck couple can squeeze in. Like deciding between green beans and spinach, both of which look very tasty at the cafeteria, families often have to make choices between choir practice and committee work, between teaching Sunday school and serving on the presbytery or vestry.

All but four of the couples we interviewed considered themselves to be "active" churchgoers, yet they showed a remarkable variety in the amount of time they spend each week on church projects. Some said they still managed to put every cafeteria item available on their tray; others showed how they honed in on what activities were most important to them and made the most of the limited church time they had. Still others talked about which areas they had cut back in when they had gone from a one- to a two-paycheck lifestyle.

## "How Could We Be More Active?"

A large black clock ticked away almost symbolically above the sofa where Sandra and Curtis Lengefeld sat as they discussed their role as a two-paycheck family in the church. The ticking clock was a reminder of the juggling act the Lengefelds do each week to make room for the activity they consider most important to their lives.

"How could we be more active than we are?" asked Sandra, a school teacher, when we quizzed her about what limitations having two outside jobs placed on their church activities. "I don't feel my job has kept me from doing anything there. Oh, I might visit people in my class more if I were at home during the day. But I really don't think Curtis and I would do anything different than what we do right now."

As we have mentioned earlier, the Lengefelds have the added complication of Curtis's shift work at a petroleum company. His erratic schedules mean that some Sundays he comes in from work just before time to teach his class. But their list of church involvements belie such a busy work schedule. Both Sandra and Curtis sing in their Baptist church's choir. Curtis is a deacon, and is on the church's transportation committee. He was chairman of the prayer committee for the church's recent revival. On weeks when he works the night shift, he often drops by the church during the day to help with odd jobs or to arrange chairs in his Sunday school classroom. Sandra directs a Sunday school class for third graders.

In addition to these activities, the Lengefelds regularly attend church on Sunday morning and evening, and on Wednesday nights. They are clearly a family who pull out all the stops for church, and who refuse to let jobs outside the home stand in the way.

A similar response came from Lou and James Barron, a black husband and wife team who were members of an Episcopal church noted for its racial mixture. When asked about their level of church activities, Lou and James took turns quickly listing their memberships and involvements. Listening to their responses was like watching a tennis match, as answers bounced back and forth between husband and wife in rapid-fire order.

*Lou:* "We attend every Sunday, and we both teach Sunday school."

*James:* "I teach the junior high age group."

*Lou:* "I teach fourth and fifth graders."

*James:* "I'm an usher, and I supervise the other ushers."

*Lou:* "I'm a lay reader."

*James:* "Both of us are on the education committee."

*Lou:* "Our son Jimmy is an acolyte."

*James:* "On an average week, we're at church two nights a week, plus Saturday and Sunday."

Not a bad showing, when you consider that Lou holds down a full-time job as accounting supervisor with a large oil company and James is a bailiff in a state district court.

Like the Lengefelds, the Barrons said they doubt they could be more active in church, even if only one of them worked outside the home. Lou bemoaned only one fact: she felt she could use a little more time to prepare her Sunday school lessons. But that regret obviously was not enough to make her feel inadequate to teach. She accepted the limitation and persevered anyway.

## Projects That Are Short-Term

We felt fortunate to find Janet and Clarence Zaozirny at home and not at their farm some seventy-five miles away on the warm Sunday afternoon in January when we arranged our visit. The Zaozirnys divide their attentions between two Lutheran churches—a large suburban one in the city where they live, and a small one in the farming community where they retreat with their two children as often as they can.

The Zaozirnys work hard during the week—he as a computer manager, and she as a counselor with cancer patients. "We feel like when the weekend comes, we deserve a real break," said Janet. So a few years ago they bought their rural property and are currently working to improve the house that stands on it.

When the Zaozirnys started listing their church activities, their list at first seemed almost as staggering as the Barrons' and the Lengefelds'. Clarence is an usher, has been chairman of the auditing committee and helped with the family life program at their large Lutheran church in the city. Janet teaches Vacation Bible School and was decorating chairman for the church's annual Christmas party.

Yet, on closer examination, we could see that each of their activities is a short-term project. Janet can immerse herself for several weeks planning how she will decorate the parish hall for Christmas, but once the holiday banquet is over, her commitment has passed. Likewise, Vacation Bible School takes up several weeks of her time during the summer, but does not require the long-term, Sunday-after-Sunday extraction of energy teaching Sunday school does. Clarence's ushering could also be done on a flexible basis.

By choosing activities in this manner, the Zaozirnys could remain active members in their urban Lutheran church without giving up their cherished freedom to spend a few weekends a month on their farm, where they escape work pressures. The Zaozirnys have found a solution which enables them to plug in with some vital church activities without signing their lives away in the process.

Presbyterians Barbara and Terry Myers have adopted a similar practice. Terry, a mail carrier, is an elder in their local congregation. He is chairman of the stewardship committee and also chairs a committee for their local presbytery. Barbara, a bookkeeper, attends the church ladies' group, where she is spiritual life chairman.

The Myers say they try to attend church as often as possible, which usually means most Sunday mornings and about once a month for some other church activity. But, like the Zaozirnys, they steer clear of Sunday morning commitments that would tie them to a "be there or else" situation. Terry says he often must deliver mail on Saturdays, so Sunday becomes the only day the family has together. Often they go camping.

Terry's eyes twinkle unmistakably when asked about regular church attendance. "If Sunday comes and we're not there, the church won't fall down," he says.

## Social Occasions Get Scratched Off First

Royce and Skip Smith promised themselves that they would stay active in their Baptist church at all costs when Royce took her outside job as truant officer, even if that meant the furniture at home didn't get dusted every week and the cookies in the cookie jar were store-bought.

But after only a few weeks in her new position, Royce saw that the family could not keep that pledge without setting priorities. The Smiths elected to keep activities like Royce's teaching third-grade Sunday school, and teaching children's choir on Wednesday night. Skip's activities as deacon, twelfth-grade Sunday school department director, and chairman of the missions committee would not be affected either.

But they decided social gatherings would be the first to go.

"Baptists just love to eat and meet," says Royce. "They use any excuse to have a party. If it's just a social event, probably we will say no from now on. We just can't cut out anything else."

Madeleine and Mike Hamm also are less interested in including social activities in their church schedule. Madeleine, a writer, and Mike, an attorney, chose to invest themselves in supervising the weekly visitors' coffee at their Methodist church, and in serving on the evangelism committee. They feel they are "meeting a real need by performing those tasks. These are jobs that other people have been reluctant to take," says Mike.

Madeleine says she has been tempted to attend the women's mission circle, which meets at night to permit women who work outside the home to participate. "But mostly the women who attend these things have social needs that are not being met elsewhere," she says. "A woman who works usually does her socializing during the day, and doesn't have the crying desire to be with other adults, in the same way a woman who was home all day with children would. I consider that my time can be used more profitably at church in other areas."

## Ministries Outside the Church

There are many ministries outside the walls of a particular church which can be performed by laypeople. Several of the couples we interviewed said they felt they could give as much of themselves in these programs as they do through regular church programs.

Consultants Mary Frances and Mark Henry regularly turn down requests to teach Sunday school at their Presbyterian church, although they are always on top of the list of potential teaching draftees. They have limited their church involvement in order to have time for the small intergenerational groups that they organize to bring people of all ages together in a time of sharing and personal growth.

The Henrys' groups are not official church-sponsored activities, since many people who are not members of the Henrys' church may attend. Yet the Henrys feel that conducting these groups, plus training other people to start similar groups in their geographic areas, is their most effective ministry at this point. "This is the area of the church where we can best contribute," says Mary Frances.

Kay, because she grew up in a church that had a strong missions emphasis, longs to have time to attend Baptist Young Women, the church's missions program. But she feels she cannot spare even one week night out because of her work schedule and home demands. So Kay has made a point in the past year to write regularly for the national Baptist magazine published for this group. Her articles outline how she views her journalism career as a ministry. "The last time they asked me to come [to a Baptist Young Women meeting], I told them that my writing for the magazine would have to be my contribution to church missions for the time being," she says.

Jean Storm, a Presbyterian and a home economist, has

a similar philosophy. She has chosen, for now, to make her main contribution through vocational activities outside the church. "I feel like what I'm doing is church work," she says. "In my classes, I teach people that we are all beautiful. I know the source of what I teach. I'm doing much more good than if I were at church all the time."

## A Hodgepodge of Criteria

Other couples had criteria that made equally good sense to them about what church activities to leave out and keep in. Debbie Lobaugh, a secretary, said she deliberately chose to teach Sunday school in her Baptist church to third and fourth graders because teachers in this age group are not required to attend teachers' meetings on Wednesday nights. She said it would be more necessary to go on Wednesdays if she taught high school students or adults, so therefore she purposely picks the lower grades.

Counselor Lavonia Duck said she agreed to teach a Sunday school class at her Baptist church only if she could cultivate members of the class to do outreach and plan parties—sideline tasks that often involve much of a teacher's time. "I told the church leaders I could teach, but I couldn't do much else," she says.

## Where Attending Worship Is Key

For a handful of couples, just attending regular Sunday morning worship is crucial, even if all other projects have to be weeded out for the time being.

Dana and Red Gordon consider it an accomplishment if they can only make it to weekly worship services at their Disciples of Christ (Christian) congregation. For now, even attending Sunday school or an occasional fellowship dinner is out of the question.

Since the birth of their daughter Sara, Dana, an executive secretary, and Red, a manager of financial accounting, feel that any spare moments should be devoted to their baby. Dana and Red both are required to work one Saturday a month, and they must fight heavy rush hour traffic to get home in the evenings. Dana arrives home about 6:30 P.M., and Red gets there about 7:15 P.M. To rush off to a weeknight church activity, or to spend even one hour preparing a Sunday school lesson, for them seems like an imposition, especially when they see their child so little.

"There are some things [at the church] we would like to someday get into," said Red. "There will be a time we can do them." But for now, just showing up for church on Sundays for the worship hour is their major priority.

## By Whose Definition?

One phenomenon we noticed in surveying couples about their degrees of activity in church was that the definition of "active" varied with the denomination and the particular congregation of which each couple was a part. This is an important fact for couples who are engaged in the delicate process of setting priorities and choosing activities to consider.

When we asked pastors or church leaders about various outstanding two-paycheck families in their groups, they chose couples who would be considered "active" by the standards of that particular congregation.

But we found that a couple who would be considered highly active in a Lutheran Church would be thought almost sluggish and lackadaisical in a Church of Christ. This is largely because "active" to a Church of Christ person means attending Sunday evening and Wednesday night services as well as attending to Sunday morning duties. To a Lutheran, whose church usually has no services outside the Sunday morning worship hour, having some role on Sunday morning and perhaps serving on one church committee would be quite sufficient to put that couple in the active category.

Furthermore, degree of activity can sometimes vary from church to church within a denomination. For example, Kay and I would be considered active in our Baptist congregation for merely being regulars at Friday night worship and for planning an occasional social or teaching an occasional seminar, because our particular church is the type that offers a wide variety of programs and expects individuals to choose among them. In a Baptist church across town, however, we would be considered backsliders if we were not faithful attenders at Sunday night worship as well as the midweek prayer service, and did not have a string of committee or teaching posts attached to our names.

The pastors of some congregations were grateful if a husband and wife attended only twice a month, but pastors of other congregations frowned on a family who did not literally meet the trite-but-true qualification of being at church every time the doors were open.

We do not advocate that a two-paycheck family join a particular church just because they think that group will make fewer demands on them. "Getting off lighter" is not a good reason to join one congregation over another. But it is absolutely essential that the couple be aware that "active" depends on who's defining the terms.

## It's Not the Pastor's Decision

The type of person who likes for someone else to make decisions for him or her should skip the rest of this chapter and simply ask his or her clergyman how much time should be spent in church.

But a word of warning here: The pastor likely will think of his or her own needs first when giving an answer. He or she will readily pull out of the hat a long string of committee, teaching, visiting, writing, and cooking assignments, and will eagerly stick the inquirer in any available slot. Who can blame the pastor? That's part of his job—to keep the church moving, vital, and growing. A pastor who has all the places of service in his church filled either is ready to retire, has lost interest in the ministry, or hasn't learned the secret of building a vibrant, exciting congregation.

However, most pastors prefer that a member have an idea of where and how he or she can best be of service. Nothing troubles a pastor more than appointing people to committees, only to have them resign a month later because that appointment has overloaded their schedules. And teachers who quit in mid-quarter just because they didn't realize how much preparation was involved in readying a Sunday school lesson can be a real problem to church leaders.

Couples who want to do themselves, their church, and their minister a favor will sit down and map out how much time they can give and where they can best plug in to their church. And they won't let anyone else make that decision for them.

## Do Some Computations

In order to solve this sometimes tricky problem in their lives, the working husband and wife must ask themselves two questions: (1) how much time *can* they afford to spend on church and church-related activities? and (2) how much time do they feel they *need* to spend on church and church-related activities? These are two separate questions. One involves a practical look at the two-paycheck couple's schedule; the other involves a serious review of their spiritual and emotional needs for church involvement.

These are questions each couple must answer for themselves; we can only offer some guidelines to use in considering them.

To answer the first question, begin by honestly reviewing all that you do in a week. Get a legal-sized yellow pad and write everything down if possible. How much time do you spend at work? How much time do you spend on the freeway commuting to and from your job? How much time do you spend doing home-maintenance tasks—laundry, marketing, cleaning, cooking? How much time do you and your spouse need to be together? How much family time do you need with children? How much sleep is imperative? Don't forget time for leisure or for puttering around the house, if that is your style. Try to figure in all the ways you spend your time. Don't bother totaling up your hours; this list is not intended to be a legalistic computation. It is simply a tally to give you a more accurate idea of where your time goes in the course of a week.

Now, surveying the list, ask yourself: Am I spending time on other areas of my life at the expense of the church? Be honest. Are you investing hours on the golf course that could be used to prepare a Sunday school lesson? Could you better use the hour that you spend doing needlepoint on a weeknight to call members of your Sunday school class and invite them to a social? Is it really necessary to wax your car once a month on Saturday afternoons, or could you better use that time to help out on the church's finance committee? We wouldn't begin to contend that car waxing, needlepoint, or golf aren't worthwhile ways to spend time. They may be very necessary diversions in your hectic life. The purpose here is to review how you apportion your life in relation to your church commitments. (In Chapter 8, we'll offer some suggestions on time management that may help you make better use of your day and therefore provide more time for church in your schedule, if that is your goal.)

Now, we turn to the next question: How much time do you feel you *need* to spend on church-related activities?

Again, this question is highly personal, because it requires some introspection about what the church means to you. It provides a framework for deciding how important it is to squeeze in church activities.

One way you might approach this subject is to "brainstorm." Agree before you start that you are merely tossing out for discussion any idea about church attendance that comes to your mind. All suggestions are fair game: in brain-storming, nobody's answer is right or wrong. No matter how preposterous your idea may seem to you, it's acceptable in a brainstorming session.

First, kick around the idea of how you would feel if you attended church every night of the week. Then turn to the other extreme: talk about how you would feel if you attended worship on Sunday morning only once or twice a month. Discuss all the other options in between, until you begin to have a feel for what is right for each of you and for you as a couple.

Recognize that in your discussion you'll encounter road-blocks. You may be tempted to settle for an answer based on how often you attended church as a child. Even though circumstances are entirely different now, you may think you must attend Sunday evening worship services just be-cause you never missed Sunday night church when you were a youngster. Or you may reach an answer based on how much you feel your mother wants you to attend church as an adult, or based on how involved your best friends are. But remember that your task is finding out what you as a couple need and feel called to give; this answer can't be based on what anyone else thinks or desires for you.

While you're brainstorming, you might want to review Chapter 2 of this book and reflect on why you go to church in the first place. In the same vein, talk about how much time you feel the Bible recommends you spend on church activities.

Once you've reached an answer, then look back at your written list of where your time goes. Are there some trade-offs you should be making? Do you spot some time-wasters in your schedule that could be eliminated to make room for that church bazaar you feel you need to help with? Remember, the converse could be true, too. You could find that you are spending too many week nights doing dead-end church committee work when family time at home is going begging. You may also be the type of person who feels totally fulfilled just by attending weekly Mass or monthly communion. Or you may think baking cookies for an occasional youth fellowship is ample contribution. But with your time allotments down on paper and your needs out on the table, you can now begin to deal with the matter of putting first things first.

## "There Will Be a Time"

But what if your schedule is tighter than a drum and church must take a very low priority? A few pages back, we quoted Red Gordon as saying, "There are some things [at church] we would like to someday get into." The Gordons have a small child and are now limited to giving church only one hour a week; the Sunday morning worship time is all they feel they can possibly squeeze in. But the Gordons are keeping a sharp eye out for the day when job demands ease, or when their daughter is older and is spending more time at church in youth activities. They will then feel more free to teach a Sunday school class, or to attend a committee meeting on a work night.

Kay's goal at church is to someday be a first-rate Sunday school teacher for young married couples—the same kind of conscientious teacher as Jane, the pastor's wife we described earlier. When we have our own family brainstorming sessions about church involvement, she regularly comments, "Someday I'm going to be a Sunday school teacher and do it right." By that, she means she will conduct a rigorous program of visiting each couple once a month, phoning or writing absentees weekly, hosting dynamite parties, writing personal notes of encouragement to class members, spending several hours a week researching lesson materials and patterning herself after Sunday school teachers she has known to be effective role models.

But realistically, she knows that she will not be able to tackle this goal until the day she takes a sabbatical from work, or possibly the day when our son is no longer a preschooler and his world is less parent-oriented. Others perhaps are waiting until they finish an apprenticeship at work, or until they are no longer expected to work overtime at their jobs.

Some people would find themselves guilt-riddled with this attitude, feeling that God doesn't deal in "somedays" and expects his children to not put off until tomorrow. But I think Kay's answer is a healthy approach: "God accepts us with our limitations at each stage in our lives. Just as a newborn can't tie his shoes or slice his meat, God knows and accepts our natural limitations until we are free to do more."

## Know Your Own Abilities

If your tally sheet and your needs assessment have shown that you should spend more or less time at church, how do you figure out what to take on or leave out? First, decide what you do best. If you're the type of person who spends hours struggling with the checkbook and can never seem to make it balance, you know that serving on the church finance committee is not your cup of tea. If you'd rather die than speak in front of a group, shy away from teaching a Sunday school class. On the other hand, if you're happiest with a telephone receiver in hand, you might consider being an outreach leader.

The church needs a variety of talents to carry out the full work of the body of Christ. Paul describes this unity through diversity in 1 Corinthians 12:12–26:

> For just as the body is one and has many members, and all the members of the body, though many, are one body, so it is with Christ. For by one Spirit we were all baptized into one body—Jews or Greeks, slaves or free—and all were made to drink of one Spirit. For the body does not consist of one member but of many. If the foot should say, 'Because I am not a hand, I do not belong to the body,' that would not make

it any less a part of the body. And if the ear should say, 'Because
I am not an eye, I do not belong to the body,' that would
not make it any less a part of the body. If the whole body
were an eye, where would be the hearing? If the whole body
were an ear, where would be the sense of smell? But as it is,
God arranged the organs in the body, each one of them, as
he chose. If all were a single organ, where would the body
be? As it is, there are many parts, yet one body. The eye cannot
say to the hand, 'I have no need of you,' nor again the head
to the feet, 'I have no need of you.' On the contrary, the parts
of the body which seem to be weaker are indispensable, and
those parts of the body which we think less honorable we
invest with the greater honor, and our unpresentable parts are
treated with greater modesty, which our more presentable parts
do not require. But God has so composed the body, giving
the greater honor to the inferior part, that there may be no
discord in the body, but that the members may have the same
care for one another. If one member suffers, all suffer together;
if one member is honored, all rejoice together.


Those scripture verses contain a message that all Christians need to understand. God has not given to any one
of us all the talents necessary to operate the church. Only
in a group of people are all the talents that are necessary
available. In more practical language: If you're a musician,
don't try to be an accountant unless you have that talent,
too. Don't force yourself into a mold that isn't really you.
There are plenty of other places of service you can discover
if you do some creative thinking.

If teaching a Bible class is your thing, be sure you plug
into an age group that you can relate to. Don't sign up to
teach five-year-olds if you can't stand being around kids.
Don't volunteer to work with the elderly unless you know
you have a natural rapport with seniors. Think back on
your previous church experience—in what areas have you
been happiest and felt most useful? Perhaps that will give
you an idea as to where you should serve.

Also, consider the type of job you hold during the work

week. If you teach junior high English five days a week, you may recoil when you see another teen-aged face on Sunday morning and may appreciate teaching adults. If you spend all week juggling the company's books, you may want to have a total change of pace, like the evangelism committee, in your church life.

You'll begrudge the time less and be more likely to make room in your schedule for church if your church duties come about because you feel you need them, you enjoy them, you feel useful, and you feel they are what God wants you to do. Only under those conditions can a church job be a benefit and not a burden to a two-paycheck family.

# 5. Learning to Say No

We had invited Rhonda and Doug to attend our annual Christmas party for a few special friends. We had purchased tickets to the best church Christmas program in town and had planned a party afterwards at our home. Since Rhonda and Doug were relatively new acquaintances, we were anxious to introduce them to others in our immediate circle of friends.

To our surprise, Doug called a few days later to decline. "Our schedule is so hectic right now; we are simply overloaded with Christmas activities," he said. "We'd really enjoy visiting in your home and getting to know you and your friends better. But I'm afraid we need to spend that evening with our children; we'll have to say no this time."

I expected to be disappointed as I hung up the telephone. But I told Doug goodbye with an entirely different feeling: it was the nicest turn-down I had ever heard in my life.

Doug offered no excuse, such as another party or a previous engagement; his response was straightforward and simple. And I did not feel insulted or hurt; his warm and sincere reply conveyed the message that our friendship was important and that they looked forward to a more uncomplicated time when we could be together.

During the time we've known Rhonda and Doug, they've probably turned down more invitations to our home than they have accepted. Yet we've never for one moment felt we were being rebuffed in our overtures or friendship. Doug has the ability—or gift—to say no skillfully. In discussing this trait, Doug says he has not acquired it easily. But over the years, he has had to learn how to set boundaries on his time.

Doug's gift for saying no gracefully is one that every two-paycheck couple needs to acquire. In order to pull off their balancing act—jobs, marriage, children, and church—members of the two-paycheck family will probably find themselves with more time conflicts than will the average person. Except for a few unusual couples, most people will not be able to accept every invitation, every assignment, every appointment that comes along. Learning to say no properly and judiciously can help make the difference in successfully including the church in a two-paycheck life-style.

In the last chapter, we discussed learning to set priorities at church. A husband and wife may determine their needs and set their goals, but that will not stop the telephone from ringing with additional requests for church work to be done. Having to say no to projects or activities is an ongoing experience that does not cut off magically just because a person has made it known that she would rather sing in the choir instead of lead a missions group, or that she would rather bake cakes for the church bazaar instead of teach Sunday school.

## Jesus Knew the Technique

In a sermon he once preached, our former pastor John R. Claypool talked about the necessity for every Christian, not just two-paycheck couples, to learn when to say yes and when to say no. Claypool said it is just as wrong to be "overinvolved in too many good causes" as it is to be "underinvolved and irresponsible."

When one is involved in too much, "life then degenerates

into a frantic blur, with you dashing from place to place and never really doing anything the way it should be done or having time to enjoy what you are doing," he said.

Jesus knew how to say no and did not permit any other human being to set his agenda, said Claypool. "Jesus had his share of people trying to get him to do this or do that, but he never capitulated to outside domination.

"In addition to maintaining control of his own existence, Jesus recognized the crucial fact that not everything that needed to be done was his to do; that is, he was able to distinguish not only between right and wrong, but also between the good and the best, between a problem that cried out for a solution and the specific shape of his own obedience in the face of all the possibilities," said Claypool.

As an example of how Jesus could say no when it was best for him, Claypool cited the eleventh chapter of the Gospel of John. In that chapter, Jesus was summoned to Bethany where his good friend Lazarus was dying. Lazarus' friends urged Jesus to hurry, but he waited a full two days before leaving for Bethany. Claypool said, "Jesus did not jump like a puppet when his string was pulled. Why? Because there was a 'best' for him that took precedent over this more obvious 'good.' He had a task to perform that was more crucial than sitting by Lazarus' side."[1]

## Sometimes It's the Kindest Act

I find that saying no to a pastor or church leader is almost twice as difficult as is turning down a neighbor or even a boss. Part of this conflict comes because I know how heavily a church relies on volunteer labor. I've been in lay leadership positions in churches, and I have felt let down when others have said no to me. When one is in the position of having to ask, the nos hit hard, and I try to remember that when I come to a minister with a turn-down.

But over the years, I've learned that a refusal is sometimes the kindest act I can make—for myself, my marriage, my children, my church, and even my pastor. Yes, even my pastor.

Pastors do not like to hear the word no from their parishioners. In fact, I've heard sermons on why lay people should do just the opposite—say yes at every opportunity. I agree with many underlying principles in those sermons: lay people are the backbone of the church; lay people can best do the work of the ministry in the world; without lay people, the church would surely die.

But if a person accepts a church task only half-heartedly, then he or she will never fulfill that job with the same energy and zeal that he would give it if he were thoroughly committed. It will not be a case of "Give of your best to the master," as the familiar hymn urges. If a person says yes to a church responsibility without really wanting to do the job, he or she often will wind up resigning from the job before it is completed. And that sort of approach helps no one.

It seems that Jesus' words in Matthew 5:37 have some application here: "Let what you say be simply 'Yes' or 'No'; anything more than this comes from evil." In this verse, Jesus was talking specifically about oaths. But I see a meaning that transcends the issue of swearing and applies to our communications with one another at church as well as in every day life. We should let our yesses mean yes and our nos mean no. To say yes when we really mean no is not helpful; it is downright deceptive and can sometimes cause more problems than saying no in the first place.

Jackie, a college student in a Sunday school class we taught years ago, struggled with this problem more than any other person I can think of. Bright, clever, creative, and energetic, Jackie was an artist, and he could turn a publicity poster into a museum piece. Any Sunday school director would envy having Jackie on his team when it came time to plan a party or a special event. The only trouble was that Jackie habitually overloaded himself with too many tasks. As a result, few of them were ever completed.

Although we knew his track record was less than perfect, we accepted Jackie's offer to handle publicity for a Halloween party we were planning for the college students that year. Because the party was scheduled for just after midsemester exams, Jackie's role was crucial, because we would not be seeing many of the students between the time we first planned the party and the party itself. Kay and I were uncertain that Jackie had time to fulfill his obligation, but he cheerfully assured us that he would "take care of everything." His job was to draw and mail out invitations to every member of the rather large class, to make clever posters to hang on the bulletin boards at his college campus, and to make special announcements during Sunday school class time.

As the date for the party neared and few people had responded, we began to suspect the worst: Jackie had let us down. There were no postcards, no posters, no special announcements—except what we managed to throw together at the last minute. Only a handful of students showed up at a party we had worked very hard to host. When confronted, Jackie apologized and said he had been too busy to work in the publicity.

What agony we would have been spared had Jackie merely said no in the first place. Scrambling to find a substitute artist—even someone with less talent than Jackie—would have been easier than planning a party no one attended.

All of us have been in Jackie's shoes at some point in our lives. I once agreed half-heartedly to chair a search committee for a new minister of music at our church. After only a few meetings, however, I quickly saw I was the wrong person for the job. As someone who hardly knows Bach from Spock, I was the only nonmusician on the six-member committee. Most of the time, I could barely "plug in" when these knowledgeable people discussed cantatas, robes, graded choirs—all their goals for the music program of the church. Embarrassed to abandon the ship in mid-course, I stuck out my chairmanship post for nearly a year, until the committee finished its work. But I was miserable the entire time and realized the kindest act I could have performed was to turn down the appointment initially, so that a person experienced in the music field could have been committee chairman.

At another point, Kay and I were recruited to team-teach a Sunday school class of young married couples. All along, we knew that something didn't "fit" about this particular appointment; although it was hard to define, both of us had a sense that we would not mesh with this group of young people. After three months of teaching, Kay and I knew we had made a serious mistake. We soon resigned— a very painful thing to do—and the pastor at midyear had to conduct a search for new teachers. Our better judgment told us to say no before we took the job. Yielding to that inner voice would have saved us, the pastor, and the church, much anguish.

## Don't Forget to Say, "Tell Me More"

We've also said yes at times when we should have said, "tell us more so we can make a wise choice."

When we moved to Houston a decade ago, we were child-less and eager to find a church where we could become involved in teaching Sunday school. The Monday after we settled on a church and joined, our wish was answered: the pastor called me at the office to see if Kay and I would team-teach a Sunday school class for single adults. I was so eager to have a place of service that I accepted immedi-ately, almost before I had time to find out the meeting place or the group's name. In my haste, I failed to ask enough questions. It didn't take long for us to learn that we were the sixth different teaching group to undertake this assignment during the past two years. The college students in the class seemed to have a knack for "chewing up and spitting out" teachers in rapid-fire order; we quickly learned that some members had us pegged for the seventh notch on their belts. I also learned belatedly that the pastor was gravely concerned about some of the theological beliefs held by some of the members of this class. He later told me he had recruited us in hopes that we would "rein in" some of this rebellious bunch.

I might have said no had I known the full story. In retrospect, Kay and I look on this teaching assignment as a learning experience and, overall, we're glad we took it. We survived six times longer than had any teacher who had previously taught there, and to this day we still keep up contact with some of the members of that class. But saying "tell me more" before agreeing so readily might have saved us many perplexing hours while we tried to figure out this mysterious group.

Mary Frances and Mark Henry describe similar struggles in dealing with their Presbyterian congregation.

"Over the past five or six years, I've learned—painfully learned—that I would go through a cycle of accepting everything that I was asked to do and then not be able to get it all done," says Mark. "I would start getting angry. Then I would back off completely. I'm beginning to learn to say no when I'm first asked now. When someone says, 'Can you serve on this church committee?', I now just say 'I'd rather not. I've got too many things going. That would overload me. Let someone else get the blessing this time.'"

Mary Frances said churches often pick out people as sacrificial lambs once they have shown they want to be lay leaders in the congregation. She said it's the price people pay—sometimes unfairly so—for ever volunteering the first time. "Part of my fears of saying no was that if I declined, I would not be seen in my church as a leader. My style was to get overinvolved, and then to get physically sick, so I could get out of everything."

Part of learning to say no for the Henrys has been deter-
mining what they do best and what they enjoy the least.
"The thing that really helped me has been to identify what
my gifts are," said Mary Frances. "Being treasurer of my
Sunday school class or serving on the Women in the Church
Committee are not things I do well. I'm not a good adminis-
trator. I've concluded that it is not good stewardship of
my time to get involved in some of those things."

The Henrys have one church-related problem unique to
their two-paycheck lifestyle: they operate their joint con-
sulting business, called "Growthlines," from their home.
They are therefore more readily available to church than
are some other couples. Says Mary Frances, "Because we
are at home, the church feels it is more OK to call and
say, 'Since you guys aren't doing anything, come help us
out.' It may look to someone like we're not doing anything
because it may be one of those weeks that we are staying
home doing books." Because their hours are more flexible,
"there is a real temptation to say yes everytime someone
from the church calls," she said.

## A Variety of Styles

Interviews with other couples revealed a variety of styles
for dealing with "turn-downs." Couples shared ways that
they were able to say no diplomatically without losing face
with church leaders and without losing esteem in their congregations.

When lawyer Judy Dougherty finds she must say no to
requests for help at her Catholic church, she said she tries
to soften the blow as much as possible by offering to assist
the person seeking her services. "When I can't do something,
I will often say that I will try to find someone who can
do it," she said.

Attorneys Carol and Ted Dinkins said they prefer to shoot
straight with folks at their Lutheran church who come to
them for help with activities. "If I'm not interested, I just

say I'm not interested," said Carol. "How will they ever have any feedback on their programs if I make up some excuse? It's much easier to tell them I'm not interested than to make excuses."

Methodist John Ahsmann, who with his wife Linda operates their own interior design shop, said he tries to offer a compromise if he finds he must decline a church assignment. "I tell them, 'I can't do that job, but I might consider doing this one.'"

One way Beverly Hebert solved the problem was by being less visible. When she returned to her job in public relations, she and her husband Joel, an engineer, had to cut back on their activities at their Catholic Church. "Returning to work has tremendously reduced the amount of free time I have and has made me less willing to invest time in activities I don't think serve an essential need or purpose," she said. "I've come to place more value on things like making dinner for someone who is sick, or babysitting with a friend's child, than on going to church meetings." Consequently, as Beverly became less involved, she was asked to help out less often. "Those people who are visibly involved are the ones who get asked to do more and more."

Similarly, Dr. Grover Laird, a general practitioner in the black community, said his "lack of performance in the past" keeps him from having to say no in the present, in the area of soliciting money. "I never feel comfortable in asking people for money," he said. "I just simply do not participate." Although he is involved in almost every other area of church life at his Episcopal church, Laird believes word has gotten around his congregation that he is not one to be called upon for fund-raising.

Attorneys Linda and Eric King said the best way for them to say no at their Church of Christ is "to be direct, clear, unequivocal and unapologetic. That way, we minimize our guilt feelings and communicate to the asker that we are busy and therefore must make choices, and that we are satisfied that our choices are correct," said Linda. She said their family "has learned the hard way that to overcommit one's time is to guarantee an unsatisfactory result all around—frustration, poor quality work, resentment, and anger. So where it is clear ahead of time that we won't have time to properly do something, we try to say no at the outset."

Donna Oates, a Baptist and a public school teacher, said she might say no initially, but if a church leader approached her again and was unable to find anyone for the slot, "I usually trudge forth and do it."

Bob Lobaugh said the indirect method always works best for him. "Usually something will die on the vine," said Bob, a technical sales representative for an engineering company. For example, when he is asked to attend socials at his Baptist church, he tells the caller, "If we can, we will." Then, if he and his wife Debbie can't work the party into their schedules, there are fewer hurt feelings than if he had initially bellowed out a resounding no.

Because Donna and Bob Porter's Free Methodist church is so small, each person in the congregation must carry his or her own weight. "Therefore, we seldom say no," said Donna, a teacher. "Our church is a close group, and we each know what the other person can do. You're seldom asked to do something that you can't. Normally, when you're asked, the request is stated in such a way that you feel good and are not left feeling guilty." Bob, an accountant, said church members are deliberately asked in this manner—"Do you have time to take this project on?"—instead of "Will you do this task?"

## How Work Enters In

The couples we talked with also dealt with the work-church conflict in various ways. Some indicated they would rather die than admit to a pastor or church leader that they could not teach a Sunday school class or serve on a church committee because their dual-job lifestyle had them overloaded; others said they never hesitated to tell a pastor if work was the key reason for the conflict.

The weekend we visited Royce and Skip Smith, Royce had just turned down her first church activity since taking her job as truant officer, after years of being a homemaker and being highly active in her Baptist church.

Royce said that her new job and the demanding new schedule actually had little to do with her absence at the prayer retreat for young married women her age. "My daughters had just gotten over the chicken pox; it was their first weekend to be well, and I didn't want to be away from them. But I got the impression that everyone thought it was because of my job." And because of Royce and Skip's earlier promise to themselves about never using work as an excuse, it was obvious that they would try to never let their two-paycheck lifestyle be the reason given for missing a church function.

On the other hand, Donna VanderWeide, who with her husband operates a private school, said her job is almost always the reason she has to decline a church activity or assignment at her Presbyterian congregation. "I explain my class load—that I teach morning and afternoon kindergarten with forty-six students—and the people at the church understand."

Marriage and family counselor Lavonia Duck said she is certain her widespread reputation as a career woman keeps the leaders of her Baptist church from leaning on her for excessive church involvement.

"I don't have to tell them no because of my work," she said. "The church is constantly referring [counseling] clients to me; they know that I work at least fifty hours a week, and so they don't hit me up for a bunch of extra church activities."

For Linda Ahsmann, an interior decorator and a Methodist, the decision is cut-and-dried: "I tell them I can't come because I work during the day and I need to spend time at home with my kids"—a statement that some two-paycheck couples might shy away from making because they fear the lecture that might ensue.

But Linda quickly added, "I probably would say no to some activities even if I was not working. I simply wouldn't want to be at church five nights a week, even if I had all the time in the world. If you go too much, you can get involved in the bickering. And that just kills it for you."

## Don't Abuse the Excuse

As word circulated around our church that we were writing a book on the church and the two-paycheck family, Kay was invited to speak to a morning group of Baptist Young Women. Most of these women had been full-time homemakers since their children were born, and they asked Kay to speak on the general topic of the Christian woman in the working world.

The speech received a strong reaction from this group, who complained loudly that they were tired of women who worked outside the home "using their jobs as an excuse for getting out of everything."

"I'd just like to tell them that I work, too, only my work is with me twenty-four hours a day," one homemaker said. "I feel like I'm being dumped on and discriminated against because I have to do all the volunteer jobs."

The meeting was a good sounding board to show us we must make this point: any excuse can be abused. Although being overloaded with work and short-changed on time is certainly a valid reason for turning down a request, it can also be used like the little boy crying "wolf" too many times. People who become like a tape recording with the words, "No, I can't; I work," recited over and over can lose their credibility and can give two-paycheck families a bad name in church, as well as elsewhere.

Carol Dinkins, the federal lawyer who commutes from Washington to Houston on weekends, probably has more demands on her time than do any of the other working mothers we interviewed; nevertheless, she was one of the most vocal about needing to carry her share of the load: "No volunteer project, which is what church is, can exist without 'X' number of people being willing to do 'X' number of things," said Carol.

Of course, there are working mothers who go too far in their efforts to "share the load." They always volunteer to be room mothers at school, missions leaders at church, den mothers in cub scouts—so much that they exhaust themselves and end up being ineffective at all their activities.

It is important to try to avoid either extreme—taking on too much work to "prove" something, or hiding behind the lifestyle to avoid doing a fair amount of work. A two-paycheck couple needs to figure out what their share is at church, and then do it cheerfully—not using work as an alibi unless it is the real reason for declining. If you don't like spaghetti suppers and would turn down the opportunity to sell tickets for one even if you had seven free days a week, don't claim you're refusing because you are part of a two-paycheck family. Using work as an excuse will usually backfire, eventually.

## Some Conclusions on Saying No

From our own experiences plus the responses of the couples we interviewed, we have reached these conclusions about saying no to church activities:

(1) *Try to know before you are asked which programs and activities you would like to accept and which you would like to decline.* Summertime, when many churches are usually a little more relaxed in their schedules, is a good time to plot this out. Or, if your church operates by a different calendar and makes committee appointments in the early spring or winter, try to make up your mind what your response will be before the church nominating committee approaches you. That way, your answer will be well thought out and you will save everyone's time.

(2) *Keep in mind how tight your schedule is already and what any additional responsibilities would do to your life.* If every weeknight is already spoken for—either with work, family, or outside commitments—don't delude yourself into thinking that some empty time slot is going to magically appear. Take the entire family's schedule into planning. If your wife's only night to work late is Tuesday, then consider what adding Tuesday-night choir practice would do to the already confusing atmosphere around your home.

(3) *If you feel you must say no, do it straightforwardly.* Don't beat around the bush about it. Excuses are ineffective and dishonest and sometimes they boomerang. Decide in advance how you feel about telling a church leader that you are declining because of a work-church conflict.

(4) *Say no quickly if that is the answer you intend to give.* If you're already certain you will decline, don't hedge or mislead the person who has asked you. Don't stall while you gather courage. It will only waste your time and theirs.

(5) *State clearly why you are not participating.* If you don't like the program, think it is insipid or boring or is a bad idea, follow Carol Dinkins' lead and give the real reason—but do it tactfully. Churches need feedback on whether their programs serve the needs of their people. Church leaders appreciate helpful suggestions about their programs, especially if the suggestions are given courteously.

(6) *Know your church's needs and how they best mesh with your abilities.* If your church choir is bursting at the seams while Sunday school classes are going begging, consider forgoing choir and volunteering to help with Sunday school.

(7) *Develop your own personal prayer and devotional life in such a way that you are attuned to God's leading about how you can best use your gifts.*

## How to Handle Guilt

The popular book, *When I Say No, I Feel Guilty,* by Manuel Smith, offers some sound techniques for learning to decline. The book was based on the premise that many people say yes to things they would prefer to say no to, because they are too guilt-ridden to say how they really feel. Smith contended that such people end up feeling "walked on" by others because they have not maintained their own personal boundaries. People who have trouble saying no in other areas of their lives likely have trouble saying no at church as well. Smith's book has helpful guidelines for bringing these out-of-bounds problems in check.

It is not our aim to analyze why people feel guilty over saying no at church. But we do know that such guilt does exist, because we have experienced it ourselves. And it is often the people who are doing the most at church who feel the sharpest guilt pangs when they have to decline something.

If you are doing what you feel is right for you—given the amount of time you have available—then guilt has no place in your life. Perhaps you should instead focus on the positives—reframe the matter by looking on just how much you are contributing instead of how deficient you are. It might be helpful to repeat these words of our former pastor, John Claypool: "There is nothing I can do to make God stop loving me. There is nothing I can do to make God love me any more than he does right at this minute."[2] Going to church seven days a week will not earn God's love for you.

If you feel guilt for saying no to one particular program or request, rethink your answer and see if you still come up with a no. Lutheran Janet Zaozirny offers some good advice on this. As a counselor, Janet is trained to be aware of her feelings. She and her husband Clarence, a computer specialist, are also aware of their tight schedules. "If it were something I could do, I would," said Janet. "I want to help [at church], but if it is too much and I know I can't, then I say no. But if saying no would make me feel guilty, then I would say yes."

If you are doing as much as you can at church and still feel those guilt pangs, we suggest that you talk the matter

over with a qualified counselor or therapist who is sympathetic to your lifestyle. Don't ask a pastor who you know
is outspoken against women working or against the two-
paycheck lifestyle. He'll already have an answer waiting
before you share your concern: do more, and if you can't,
quit your job, or rejuggle your priorities. Find someone who
is willing to listen with an open mind and to work with
you on the problem.

## What if You've Already Said Yes?

Up to this point, we've concentrated on how to say no
to excessive church activities. What happens if you've already said yes and now regret it? In the beginning of this
chapter, we gave an illustration of a time we failed to say
no at the right moment. We've gotten ourselves involved
in some church programs and later realized we had made
the wrong decision.

If you are involved in a predicament like this, the first
thing to do is to accept the fact that the situation has become
more complicated than if you had said no at first. But just
because your situation is more complex doesn't mean it is
hopeless.

One question to ask yourself is, "How much longer does
this job last?" If it is only a few more weeks or months
and you think you can persevere, you might be better off
to continue it. Stick it out, and then next time practice
more restraint in saying yes.

Donna VanderWeide shared this experience: "This past
year I have refused requests to teach Sunday school and
to serve as youth division chairman. I tried to teach a seventh grade class last year, and although I finished the year,
I did not feel I gave the preparation and thought to it that
I have done in the past. It was frustrating for me not to
do the best job I was capable of doing."

If the program that you wish you hadn't so eagerly said
yes to is an open-ended commitment, or will last longer

than you feel you can tolerate, you have two choices: resign or endure. Either way is not easy. Resigning can be embarrassing and can cause hard feelings. Continuing with something you wish you hadn't gotten into can cause intense anger. We've found it is often better to offer a prayerful resignation than to smolder in resentment.

We visited Linda and Larry Calvert only a few days after he had resigned as a ruling elder at their Presbyterian church. "I'm very committed to doing a good job at whatever I do," said Larry, head of marine distribution at a chemical plant. "Unfortunately, I'm so much that way, that I do it to my own detriment. When it came down to making a choice between spending time at session meetings or spending time with Lindsay [the couple's newborn daughter], I chose to be at home. It was easier to give up being a ruling elder."

We could tell it was not easy for Larry to make this decision. Being ruling elder is a position of honor and respect afforded only to lay persons who have shown a willingness to work hard and who have a gift for leadership.

Naturally, to avoid such situations, it is best to say no in the beginning. But that cannot always be done. In Larry's case, for example, Lindsay arrived unexpectedly after he was already committed to a heavy church load. For this reason, we've found it best never to accept a role in a church program without first obtaining a clear understanding of what the task means in terms of time commitment—six months, a year or forever. Because life has a way of changing, there will always be times when you need a chance to reevaluate your commitments—and if necessary, to bow out gracefully.

# 6. Finding the Right Church for You

The first Sunday after President Jimmy Carter moved into the White House in 1977, he and his wife Rosalynn transferred their membership to First Baptist Church of Washington, D.C. The Carters said they chose that church because it was the closest Baptist congregation to their new home.

Before moving to 1600 Pennsylvania Avenue, the Carters had investigated several other Baptist churches in the Washington, D.C., area for possible membership. Probably any church in the district would have welcomed the presidential couple with open arms. But proximity to the White House was what the Carters decided would be the key factor in their selection.

The Carters may have decided to join First Baptist Church because they were accustomed to a neighborhood church, since their congregation in Plains, Georgia, also was only a short distance from their home there. Politics also may have entered the picture. Basing their selection on location was a neutral enough reason to avoid offending other Baptist churches in the area. Whatever their reasons for using proximity as the basis for their decision, it was evident that their choice was not based on happenstance but was clearly and carefully thought out.

Each family has its own reasons for choosing the church

it attends. Perhaps the friendliness of the congregation appeals to one couple. Another couple is attracted by the preaching style of the minister or the worshipful atmosphere of the service. Or perhaps, as in the case of the Carters, having a church in the neighborhood is the most compelling factor. Some people who as adults live in the town where they were reared choose to stay in the church of their childhood because of their spiritual roots and the church's familiarity. Sometimes the recommendations of friends go a long way in forming a decision. Sometimes it's merely a matter of liking one church's architecture, or its choir.

## Lifestyle as a Factor

One of the primary reasons we joined the church we now attend was our two-paycheck lifestyle. The church's schedule, programs, ministry, and attitudes are more suited to working couples than are other churches we considered. Over the years, we have discovered that two-paycheck families have unique needs that not every church is equipped to handle.

Finding a church where our lifestyle meshed with the ministry of the church was an intense pilgrimage, however, and was not without serious research and many trials and errors. During the ten years we've lived in Houston, we have been members of four different Southern Baptist congregations. Perhaps by tracing that somewhat painful history in this chapter, we can help others identify with our mistakes and avoid similar pitfalls.

When we first moved to Houston in 1972 as virtual newlyweds, we were naïve about the crucial role our two-paycheck lifestyle would play in our church life, and our criteria for finding a Houston church "home" were rather simple. Basically, we wanted (1) a large church which would offer a variety of programs, and (2) a church where we could make friends easily and become involved. Since our closest friends in Houston at that time highly recommended their church to us, and because it seemed to meet our basic guidelines, we joined up rather quickly.

After five years, we left that church for one reason: its location in relation to our jobs and home. When we joined, we had given only cursory attention to the fact that the church was completely remote from our normal patterns of movement. It was neither near our home nor near our offices. At that time, gas prices were lower, Houston's traffic was lighter, and we were childless. But the fact that church was always "out of the way" for us made it extremely hard to include church activities in our schedule. For example, we had wanted Wednesday night Bible study to be on our agenda. But the first Wednesday night we were members there, we discovered how impossible that plan would be to accomplish. We left the office late because Kay had to write a late-breaking deadline story. We raced across town through some of the worst traffic we had ever encountered and arrived after other members had finished what probably was a very tasty evening meal. (Baptist churches are usually noted for their Wednesday night suppers.) A few similar incidents like this, and we permanently scratched plans to be Wednesday night churchgoers.

As time passed, we began to discover that we never saw any of our friends from church anywhere outside of church. They all lived in neighborhoods surrounding the church, while we lived forty minutes away by car. When we planned parties for the Sunday school class we taught, members complained loudly—and justifiably so—about the driving distance to and from our home.

We took all these little disruptions in stride until after our son Matthew was born. At his birth, the pastor's wife called to tell us that the ladies of the church had decided to forgo the usual meal for a new mother that they customarily prepare, and would simply bring a gift instead, because we lived too far from the church for food to be transported easily. As we began traveling to church with a crying, hungry infant who couldn't seem to understand why he had to undergo such a lengthy wait from the time we left the church until the time we reached his food, we began to realize just how impractical our church location was. We could foresee greater problems when Kay returned to work from her maternity leave; time would be even more limited, now that we had a young child to think about. Sadly, we left the first church, determined to learn from our first series of errors.

## When Location Was the Priority

When trying to find a second church to join forces with, we decided that the Jimmy Carter criterion—a neighborhood church—was the only answer. And we found one—a large and prosperous congregation near our suburban home. We could breeze in to church in about six minutes, even if we were running late. Suddenly, we were in attendance, as the saying goes, "every time the door was open." Wednesday night suppers that had been inaccessible to us at the first locale suddenly were standard fare. Parties we tossed were well-attended since they were on everyone's beaten path; we enjoyed bumping into Sunday school class members at the neighborhood grocery; dropping by fellow church members' homes was easy since most of them lived only blocks away. We babysat for each others' children, and discussed the time when our kids would all be in the same school together. Kay and I looked forward to being able to keep up this same level of activity once she returned to work, since the church was right off the freeway between our home and office. The neighborhood church seemed the perfect answer.

But as the months passed, we began to realize that a good location could not be the sole criterion for us in finding the right church either. As we detailed in an earlier chapter, because this church was situated in a prosperous suburban neighborhood, it had on its rolls very few couples who found themselves outside the wife-at-home, husband-at-work mold. And most of our fellow church members were basically unaccepting when Kay ended her year's maternity leave six months after we became members. The church seemed to pride itself on being somewhat monoculture, and it seemed to have no room for persons who didn't fit the norm. From that experience, we learned a valuable lesson: a two-paycheck family has to choose a church with more than one factor in mind. In this case, our primary criterion for choosing—the location—contributed to its being the wrong church for us.

## A Transitional Third Church

Our third choice was a tentative, transitional one. After realizing our mistake in joining the second, prosperous suburban congregation, we were frustrated about the current situation. Admitting failure is not easy for either Kay or me. And the idea of having to join a third church in such a short period of time troubled us greatly. In one sense, I felt that my job as religion editor should somehow make me immune from such problems. After all, who should know more about churches in the Houston area than someone in my position? But on the other hand, I was still a novice at the problems that a two-paycheck family would encounter in a church. It never occurred to me that a lifestyle could limit one's range of church selection in quite the way ours had.

Fortunately, the next solution came quickly. The suburban church where we had been members was starting a new mission congregation fifteen miles from our home, in a small town west of Houston. The church was begging for volunteers to help get the new congregation going. We felt a theological kinship with the young pastor who was in charge of spearheading the mission, and we were intrigued by the idea of being part of something new, of being in on the formation of a church from its inception. And we hoped that our being charter members of a new congregation would give us a pivotal role in helping design a church body where two-paycheck couples like ourselves could fit in. Somehow, we believed that a fresh new church that had no history would not be ingrained with the old stereotypes we found in our last church experience.

In the beginning, when the church met only on Sunday mornings during its organizational phase, the new situation seemed to be working out well. But as the church grew, its leaders became anxious to add just as many programs as possible to the agenda, so that it eventually would offer all the services of the suburban church that had founded it. Since it was only a "baby" church with a few key members at that point, we were asked to sit on virtually every committee, to be present at every meeting, to help set up chairs, to teach every Sunday, to literally hold up the organization during those crucial early days. When the church got around to starting a Wednesday night program, the pastor insisted that all teachers attend regularly. Weekly Tuesday night visitation programs also were virtually mandatory for the small band of leaders. Such heavy requirements would have been difficult to work into our two-paycheck lifestyle, even if this church had been two blocks from our home. But here, again, distance became a problem. Because it was a mission church, our new congregation was situated in a remote area of town where people were just starting to move and develop a neighborhood. It was even farther removed from our beaten path than was the first church we attended, and it necessitated a fifteen-mile drive beyond our home into a sparsely populated rural area.

In our idealism, we had hoped to help shape this new church into a body of people more tolerant of other lifestyles, and in a sense, this was happening, since the mission was situated in a new part of town with many different types of people—including several two-paycheck families—joining the church roster. But the ambitious young pastor, consumed with his goals of building one of Houston's fastest-

growing congregations in a brief time span, was unrespon-
sive to our complaints about time pressures. In his determi-
nation to get his church off the ground, he was unable to
understand why a lifestyle such as ours should be a valid
reason to say no to his requests. And, in such a setting,
people who did say no found themselves sticking out like
sore thumbs. Most of the people who formed the fledgling
congregation were just as eager as the pastor to put the
new church on the map.

In our discouragement at seeing yet another church effort
go afoul for us, we felt at first like lashing out at the whole
situation. We were angry at the young pastor for being
so ambitious and so insensitive. Then we realized that the
problem was basically ours and not his. In our eagerness
to be part of a new congregation and to try to mold a
new church to fit our situation, we had been very unprag-
matic. We had failed to realize that charter members of
any new body must commit themselves to be workhorses
for many, many months. Joining a new, small congregation
had made it almost imperative that we be superactive, no
matter what kind of time involvement that required. Being
a two-paycheck family is simply no excuse for missing a
committee meeting or sitting out visitation when a church
is getting off the ground.

This time our discouragement turned to desperation as
we sat in the ashes of yet another disappointing church
experience. We were uncertain which way to turn. But this
time we had learned enough from our past three situations
to hold off leaping too quickly onto another church roster.
This time, we decided, we would make a thorough review
of our situation—our problems and our possibilities. If a
denominational switch was in the offing, we wanted to
study that, too.

I want to emphasize that, despite our discouragement,
at no time did we ever consider dropping out of church
altogether, or becoming stay-at-home church members.
Many times people are too eager to "throw the baby out

with the bath water" after one church effort goes awry. Church was important to us, and we were not willing to give up on something so valuable. So the next period of our lives we spent evaluating, pondering, and deciding which direction we would pursue next in terms of church membership. This turned out to be a time of tremendous personal, spiritual, and marital growth for us. Walking through the fire to hammer out a solution gave us a chance for some significant introspection that we sorely needed in order not to "bomb out" again.

## With God's Help

In our family, we have developed a regular nightly devotional time. As Matthew goes to bed, the three of us gather in his room, and each of us tells one thing to be thankful for that day. The topics range from new kittens, to a play experience with a friend, to a long-awaited letter, to safety throughout the day. At these sessions, we also talk about things we need to pray for—people who are sick, needs in our own lives. After we have expressed those thoughts, we hold hands and one of us voices the prayer. During the time that we had decided we must again look for a new church, this item took top priority on our prayer list. We asked for God's help in the decision-making process, and prayed that this go-round, we would have added wisdom to make the right choice for all concerned. I often use the hours that I jog in the mornings as an opportunity for personal devotions. During this transition period, my only prayer seemed to be for God's guidance in leaving one church and finding another.

Another technique that had always seemed to help us was list-making. From the beginning of our marriage, when we had had to make a major decision on whether to live in Houston or Louisville for our first permanent jobs, we had always relied on lists weighing the pros and cons of each alternative. So now, feeling that we were finally experienced enough in church-shopping to know that we must select one based on all our needs and not just a few, we came up with this list of "musts":

(1) We needed a church that was close enough to our daily routine so that we could attend easily without spending too many anxious hours in the traffic.

(2) We needed a congregation large enough that it did not rely on a faithful few people to do all the work.

(3) We needed a congregation in which our two-paycheck lifestyle, if not the norm, could at least be tolerated and accepted.

(4) We needed a church located close enough to home so that we could expect to encounter at least a few of the members in our comings and goings.

We agreed that there would be no hasty decision this time. We could explore all our options and move our membership to another church only when we found one where we thought we would be happy for as long as we remained in Houston.

There were some definite guilt pangs as we embarked on this journey. At first blush, it seemed almost unfathomable that we were in the process of choosing our fourth church in such a relatively brief time. Being itinerant churchgoers was not our style; we were much more comfortable with putting down roots in a situation and sticking it out through thick and thin. Our personal history during twelve years of marriage was evidence of that tendency. All but two of those twelve years had been spent in the same city, working at the same jobs and living in the same neighborhood. In no other aspect of our life together had we experienced such relocation. So we were in for a good bout with the guilties—the "What's wrong with us?" syndrome—about our seeming inability to settle down in a church.

Yet, in working through these thoughts, I remembered that many of the students with whom I had attended seminary a decade earlier currently were moving to their third and fourth pastorates. For them, changing church situations was considered to be a feather in their caps, because ostensibly each move brought for them greater opportunities for service, greater chances to use their gifts.

Furthermore, we were beginning to grasp a new image of ourselves as a truly "special needs" couple who could not simply move into a town, plunk down our membership in the local Baptist church, and be happy. We were beginning to catch a glimpse of the fact that two-paycheck families do have some special requirements that must be met before they will mesh with a church, in the same way that a concert violinist could not expect to fulfill his potential in a town where the only cultural outlet was a community band. When we were finally able to look at the matter in this kind of light, we were able to shed the guilties and move on with a fresh sense of commitment to the task.

## The Search Begins

Our next step was to make a list of possibilities. Here, I decided to bring some of my skills into play, since during my years as religion editor I have written stories about almost every church in town. As we made our list, I searched my memory about these churches. Which were the most innovative? Which had pastors who might be most in tune with our situation? As we compiled our list, we did not limit ourselves to churches in the Southern Baptist tradition. Perhaps by widening our scope to include other denominations, we thought, we would be more likely to find a place where we would fit. In my dealings with other Christian faiths, I had learned that God is alive and active in the hearts of people with all kinds of denominational labels— Methodists, Presbyterians, Episcopalians, Catholics, Baptists, Lutherns. Although Kay and I had both been reared with Southern Baptist traditions and theology, we decided we would try to look at each choice without sectarian prejudice.

After some serious reflection, we pruned our list to five

churches we considered the most likely candidates, and we were about to start surveying each one by a personal visit. Then suddenly I had a brainstorm. Why not again use my skills and resources as a newspaper reporter by writing a story about churches and two-paycheck families? I decided that if we were having this much trouble finding the correct church home because of our lifestyle, there surely must be other couples in town frustrated by the same situation. Where had they found an answer? It occurred to me that I could write a useful story about a trend in churchgoing and help solve our dilemma at the same time.

To begin my research, I zeroed in on Houston's South Main Baptist Church, a large downtown congregation that has developed a national reputation for its ministries to single, divorced, and remarried persons. Since South Main was noted for being sensitive to lifestyles not inside the mainstream, I was curious to see how this innovative congregation dealt with two-paycheck families in its midst, and how those families felt received by the church. Dick Stafford, the church's minister to adults, eagerly agreed to round up five two-paycheck couples for me to interview. We set the interview time for the following Wednesday night in the church's conference room.

I had originally planned to attend the interview alone and to give Kay a report afterwards on what I had heard. But as time drew near for the scheduled meeting, I suddenly felt a sense of urgency that she should be there with me, so we could both hear this problem discussed first-hand. Because she would be arriving home later than usual that night, I quickly arranged a sitter for Matthew so that Kay would have no excuse for not coming along. She pulled in the driveway just as I was getting ready to leave the house, and I made my sales pitch to her. Although she obviously was weary and had not yet eaten dinner, she agreed without protest. Later, she commented that she felt as though some force was propelling her back out the door and onto the freeway that night, despite her fatigue from the day. Our bedtime prayers for a solution to our church problem were starting to be answered without our even realizing it.

In the interview, couples described their lifestyle and how the church fits into it. They were all people with whom we could quickly identify. One woman, attorney Ann Kelley, who is married to another attorney, Art Whitmer, described the church's reaction when she returned to work three weeks after the birth of her son. She said she had been braced for some sharp criticism from other church members because of the short length of time she had spent at home with her new baby. Instead, the women in her Sunday school class had been very supportive, and had even scheduled some upcoming class events at a location convenient to her office so she could dash over for a noon-time meeting.

Then Jim Blande, a traffic coordinator, and his wife Pam, a traffic planner, talked about how they never felt any pressure to attend a prescribed number of programs at the church. "People who come to this church do so because of the love for the programs of the church, the love for the fellowship within the church. The basic philosophy is that the church is very people-oriented," Jim said.

David Smith, who is in the chemical business, added, "I can't think of anyone at South Main today who feels obliged to participate in all the activities. Our pastor says even he doesn't know everything that is going on in this church. So why should I, a member, feel psychologically committed to attend everything?"

Then Robert Ketchand, an attorney, and his wife Alice, who taught accounting at a local college, threw the bombshell at us. They described the Friday Night Live program, South Main's new Friday night worship service which they said was ideally suited to the needs of two-paycheck couples. Although I had written the inaugural story about Friday Night Live, no one had ever pointed out to me specifically how it was tailor-made for two-paycheck families. Because families could participate in the full range of church activities—an evening meal, a worship service, and even a Sunday school (regular Bible study for youngsters and a series of seminars for adults)—Friday Night Live served as an alternative to Sunday worship. "We go to church on Friday night and have a family day on Sunday," Robert said. "It's like adding an extra day to our week, which is particularly important when both husband and wife work all week and need extra time to spend with their children."[1]

Kay and I glanced at each other, and I could tell she and I shared the same unspoken thoughts. Could it be that we had finally stumbled upon the answer for our own problem? We had always known about South Main's reputation in the community as being farsighted and far-thinking in attempting to reach people of all needs, but we had never thought about it in terms of being a boon for the two-paycheck family. Furthermore, since it was a downtown church, we had always automatically ruled it out, remembering our problems with driving long distances. However, the Friday night program seemed to open up a whole new realm of possibilities. South Main was only about a five-minute drive from the *Chronicle;* attending the Friday night programs would involve making a lengthy trip only one way—after church was over.

I had an irresistible urge to stand up on the conference table and shout in jubilation, but I managed to restrain myself. For the next several Friday nights, however, Kay and I were back in South Main, testing the waters for ourselves. We liked what we found, and we moved our membership several months later; since that time we have been more active in that church than we have during any previous church experience. Not only are we regulars at the Friday night program, but we also pick up Matthew from his nearby school and go as a family to the Wednesday night activities, which include children's choir and Mission Friends for Matthew. By being at church during rush hour, we manage to avoid the heavy freeway traffic on those two nights and hence arrive home much more quickly than we would driving straight home from work.

Furthermore, because South Main is an urban church and draws its members from a wide segment of the community, not just a narrow monocultured neighborhood surrounding it, people are more open-minded about different lifestyles. Instead of being offended and turned off by the fact that Kay and I both have careers, our friends at South Main are intrigued by what we do and frequently discuss our work with us. Our pastor also involves himself personally with our work through affirmative means, which we'll describe in a later chapter. And because of the flexible structure of the Friday night program, Kay and I can plug in our abilities in creative ways—leading seminars for three months at a time, planning retreats, planning after-church socials—which frees us from the strict "be at every program or else" routine we had experienced at previous churches.

Certainly no church is perfect, and we're sure there will be other times of frustration for us. But basically, we feel good about the direction our search for the right congregation took. And we learned an immense amount about ourselves, and about the special needs of the two-paycheck family, in the process.

## Other Couples Had to Search, Too!

There often were times during our pilgrimage that we surely felt we were the only couple who ever grappled with the two-paycheck/church conflict. It was refreshing, therefore, in the process of researching this book, to interview couples who had undergone similar experiences. At least one-sixth of the couples we interviewed indicated they had recently switched congregations because of their two-paycheck lifestyle, or were currently looking for a new place to put their membership.

Nora and Jim Bishop were in a period of transition in

their church life when we visited with them. Because of location, the Bishops were switching from a large downtown Methodist church to a group closer to their suburban home so that the children could be involved in more church-related activities.

But the Bishops were concerned that they would not encounter as many working couples as they had known in their downtown congregation.

"When we visited a new church recently, we looked around to see if the people 'looked like' us," said Nora, a nurse. She said it would be hard for her to be around non-professional people in a Sunday school setting.

Nora said if the family did not find what it was looking for in the first suburban church it joined, it would move on and try again until the need is met.

Jewelers Meg and Quenton Elliott had only recently joined an independent Presbyterian church when we talked with them. They had stayed out of church for several months because they had not felt comfortable with some of the attitudes they had encountered at their previous church—including a degrading view of women who worked. Because Meg was planning to return to work shortly after the birth of their son, the Elliotts had known that a church move was in the offing.

Because doing without church left an "empty spot" in their lives, the Elliotts had eventually decided to look for another congregation where they would be happy. Quenton said they had done a thorough job of checking out their new church before joining. "I did not want a church that controlled me," he said. "I want to be in control of my church situation."

Though medical students Cecilia Valdes and Mike Rutledge were referred to us by a Catholic priest, they were unsure in what denomination they would spend their married life. Their prospective marriage posed serious questions for them concerning religion. Mike had essentially left the Church of Christ seven years earlier after his parents di-

vorced and his mother returned to school and work. He
said the factors of the divorce and of his mother's career
outside the home had alienated his mother and their family
from the Church of Christ they had attended. Because of
these experiences, Mike had doubts about their two-
paycheck marriage being accepted in conservative churches
like the one he had grown up in. He said he would not
advocate that they join a Church of Christ.

Cecilia, on the other hand, wanted to remain Catholic.
She felt that by carefully choosing their friends, their priest
and their particular parish, they could hammer out a two-
paycheck lifestyle in the church of her religious heritage.
At the time we talked, Mike was lukewarm about convert-
ing, but he indicated that he would at least consider the
possibility.

## Why Some Churches Work for
## Two-Paycheck Families

Consultants Mary Frances and Mark Henry said they
believed their two-paycheck lifestyle was well received in
their Presbyterian church because "it is very accepting of
new things. It is a church where something new becomes
the norm." They said their lifestyle would probably be at
loggerheads in a more traditional church.

Madeleine and Mike Hamm said their Methodist church
works well for the two-paycheck family because "it's not
the type of church to put a guilt trip on people." Said Madeleine, a journalist, "When people come to class, we're just
tickled to death that they show up. We don't ask them
why they weren't here the previous Sunday."

Martha and Bill Haun said they believed their particular
Church of Christ congregation would be receptive of the
two-paycheck lifestyle. "This particular congregation is
very accepting of people who are not in the mainstream,"
said Bill, who is in sales with a railroad. "As a body, the

members of this particular Church of Christ are very tolerant of each other."

Linda and Larry Calvert said one of the reasons they have escaped criticism of their two-paycheck lifestyle with a small child at their Presbyterian church is because they were members of the church for so many years as a childless couple and people already identified them as professionals. "Nobody is going to approach a thirty-six-year-old career woman about returning to work after her child was born," said Linda, a college professor. "They've seen me as a professional. They know I'm old enough and settled enough to make my own decisions."

School teacher Donna Oates' personal history with her Baptist church may have helped fellow church members accept her family's two-paycheck lifestyle. Because she still lives in the same town where she grew up, many of the people she attends church with have known her since childhood. This apparently makes a big difference in what a church will tolerate.

Counselor Lavonia Duck said she believes it is easier for a two-paycheck couple to belong to a large congregation, and she and her husband Roger, also a counselor, chose their Baptist church for its size. "If you can't be there all the time, it doesn't stick out so much," she said. "They're not around counting heads all the time."

In contrast, Donna and Bob Porter believe the fact that their church is small makes it easier for their two-paycheck family to survive as church members. "Our church is like a family," said Donna, a teacher. She believes when people know one another personally and intimately, they will make a greater effort to understand why couples make certain choices about their lifestyle.

Attorneys Carol and Ted Dinkins said the educational level of their Lutheran congregation exposes members to broader perspectives. "People there want to be up with what's going on," said Carol. "Women there understand

and appreciate that their daughters will have much broader career choices than they did a few decades ago." Therefore, church members see her as a symbol of a trend in society and appreciate her. "The church is very interested in learning," said Ted.

## A Checklist

If you are already in a church that seems well-suited for your two-paycheck lifestyle, count your blessings. If you're not, don't be discouraged and—above all—don't give up the ship. We're convinced that if there was an answer for our problem, there's an answer for anybody's situation. Besides some of the obvious considerations that we've already mentioned, such as size, location, presence or lack of pressure tactics, visibility, variety of programs, and friendliness of the congregation, here are some other points you may want to consider when trying to find the right church for you.

(1) *Consider talking with someone in your community who can give you an overview about churches in town without spieling off a "party line."* In larger towns there are sometimes interdenominational agencies whose spokespeople represent a wide variety of church groups. The religion reporter on your local newspaper might be a source. Hospital chaplains, who learn to work with people of all faiths, could probably give some advice without bias. The best way to get a total view is to ask several people.

(2) *While compiling your list of possibilities, think creatively and keep your eyes open.* You may have driven past the right church for you for years and never noticed it existed. In our case, we had known about South Main since we moved to Houston, but had never perceived how it would work into our game plan until just before we joined. If you live in a small town, you may think the options are limited, and they probably are. Don't rule out a denominational switch. Sometimes people who think they could never be happy as anything

but Presbyterian, or Methodist, or Catholic, are pleasantly surprised to find how similar their beliefs are to other Christian groups. Sometimes it's easier to disagree on one or two points of dogma than it is to stay in a church where you agree on every point but feel shut out by your nonconventional lifestyle.

(3) *Meet with church officials—such as the pastor, the minister to adults, or the associate pastor—prior to joining, and don't be afraid to ask the hard questions.* Find out exactly how your lifestyle will fit into the church. Find out what will be required of you and what you can offer the church. Listen carefully to the answers you get. Had we listened more carefully and not ignored some of the answers we heard before we joined the third church—the mission—we might have thought twice. The pastor never wavered from his stated goal of turning a tiny band of souls into a large, structurally-tight congregation. He talked glowingly of the stringent commitment that would be required from each individual to make this church quickly blossom. But in our haste to link up with another church body, we closed our ears to his outline.

(4) *When considering a church, try to find out whether two-paycheck families are in the majority or in the minority.* If most families are of the traditional one-paycheck variety, decide how you will feel about being among a small handful. Talk with some of the couples to find out whether they consider themselves ostracized or part of the mainstream. Decide whether it matters to you that you are the only member of your women's mission group who can't make daytime meetings, or that you're the only member of your Sunday school class who can't attend luncheons. As a couple, will it bother you to say no repeatedly to weekend social functions because you have household or family responsibilities that come first? If so, perhaps you need to look elsewhere.

(5) *Find out whether the pastor's wife has ever worked outside the home.* Many couples we interviewed concluded that their two-paycheck lifestyle was freely accepted by their minister

because his own wife was career-oriented or had recently gone to work for pay. If the pastor is threatened or dubious about his own wife having an outside job, his attitude should raise a warning flag for a two-paycheck couple: he's likely to be uncomfortable with any working woman. However, just because a pastor's wife has no past work history should not necessarily rule out that church for a two-paycheck family. Our present pastor's wife does not hold an outside job, but his daughter is studying to be a lawyer. Our conversations with him indicate that his career-minded daughter definitely has made him sensitive to the concerns of working women. Sometimes if a church has a large staff, a husband and wife may find themselves gravitating toward one staff member who is himself a member of a two-paycheck family, even if that staff member is not the senior minister.

Of course, if the minister is a woman, the church is likely to be very accepting of two-paycheck families! Linda and John Ahsmann have found this to be the case at their Methodist church: "The associate pastor is a woman who is married and has a family. There's a certain mood that is created by that situation. It's a feeling that pervades the church that makes everyone more tolerant of working couples."

(6) *Consider the disadvantages of switching churches in the middle of a lifestyle change.* In general, we found that couples who were long-time members of their congregations seemed to fare better when the wife went back to work than did those who were newcomers to the church when the change occurred. In our case, for instance, we moved our membership to our second church during the time Kay was at home on maternity leave. The women in her Sunday school class had never known her as a professional—only as a mother who, like them, stayed at home with a child. The fact that her identity as a newspaper reporter was totally foreign to them made her desire to return to work difficult for them to grasp. Perhaps if we had been long-time members of that congregation and our identities as professionals as well

as parents had been more ingrained in people's minds, there would have been less criticism.

(7) *Don't be afraid to try and fail.* One of the hardest barriers we had to overcome was the embarrassment of repeated unsuccessful efforts. We had to come to grips with the fact that people make mistakes, even in choosing their church. A strong person learns from those mistakes, picks himself up and goes on. A religion professor at a Baptist college recently chided us by saying, "You're getting to be real church-jumpers, aren't you?" Yet this same man then went into a tirade about his present church, attacking everything from the pastor to the hymnbooks. The comments were the same he had harped on for the past ten years. It's very likely that this man has never sat down and discussed any of his complaints directly with his pastor. I'd rather confront a pastor directly about my incompatibility with his church, and then move on, than to backbite and flounder in my anger and ill-will. And just because a church doesn't suit a two-paycheck family's needs doesn't mean that that same church is wrong for all people. I have recommended each of our first three churches to numerous people in the community since we parted these congregations, even though none of the three have worked out for us. Perhaps at another time in our lives, we could have meshed with any one of them. By continuing to search for a solution, and not being deterred by charges of "church-jumping," we found our niche. We believe you can, too!

# 7. What If Your Best Friend Disagrees?

We were seated at church supper one Wednesday evening, chatting with friends while we waited for the worship service to begin in the sanctuary. A man we know only casually joined our group and began making small talk. He asked us about our work week and mentioned various stories each of us had written for the newspaper recently.

As we talked, the noise of children playing at one end of the fellowship hall grew louder and louder, until at one point it almost drowned out the adult conversations. Our five-year-old son Matthew and four friends were conducting a game of hide-and-seek behind some plastic fold-out partitions. When Kay left the table briefly to corner Matthew and his four chums and to tell them to keep the noise level down, the man remarked, "Several of us were discussing your son the other night. We just can't believe how active and boisterous he is."

Several years ago, we probably would have bristled at this offhand remark. Our defenses higher than a kite, we would have wondered why this man, certainly a mere acquaintance at best, had focused on Matthew's behavior, since our son is no more animated or rowdy than are any of the other youngsters he runs with at church, nor is he necessarily the ring leader of the group. In former times we probably would have been offended by his statement,

"Several of us were discussing your child the other night." We would have wondered why Matthew had become a subject for idle conversation among people observing him at church.

However, as we've come to better understand our role as a two-paycheck family in the church, we now assume that scenarios like this basically "go with the territory" when both husband and wife work outside the home. Because the two-paycheck lifestyle is still considered a deviation from the norm, working couples are scrutinized closely by folks who are curious about "how it all works." By its very nature, a two-paycheck family will be much more visible among peers and associates, since working couples are attempting a way of life that is still seen as a novelty of sorts. And in our case, the curiosity heightens, since our work as newspaper reporters, with bylines that appear regularly in the *Houston Chronicle*, puts us somewhat more in the limelight than the average family.

Moreover, the working mother is still seen as an anomaly to many, even though her numbers increase daily. Barbara Kaye Greenleaf, who wrote one of the first self-help books for working mothers, said, "Because old myths die hard, one of the country's oldest and most strongly-held beliefs is that the 'real mother' is the one who stays home. According to conventional wisdom, her [the working mother's] marriage will go on the rocks and her children will become emotionally deprived, depressed, delinquent and every other terrible thing imaginable."[1] Therefore, we've come to expect that when a group of people are seated at a church supper table watching five children play at the end of the room, they will naturally pay more attention to the one whose mother works full time than they will to the identical actions of other children whose mothers are home all day. The children of working mothers are being reared outside "conventional wisdom," and some people find that fact hard to forget or to shake.

Like ministers' families, two-paycheck couples constantly

find themselves living in a goldfish bowl. Suddenly the house, the children and the marriage become "fair game" for social commentary, far more than if only Dad were the breadwinner in a traditional household. This social commentary can take all kinds of forms, ranging from virtually innocent remarks like those we encountered at the church supper table to malicious back-biting and openly delivered criticism. It can arrive in the form of innuendos, lifted eyebrows or even silence—the what's-not-said that can ring so deafeningly in one's ears. One woman we interviewed was given a copy of Marabel Morgan's book, *The Total Woman*, as an overt hint from friends that she should change her ways. Another detected criticism in the way her pastor always praised women who were housewives and seemed to ignore the working women in his congregation. However it is packaged, criticism of the two-paycheck lifestyle can be a very real and painful factor in the lives of many couples. In this chapter, therefore, we will focus on ways that working couples can keep their equilibrium in the face of comments and criticism from others.

## Why Two-Paycheck Families Are Criticized

There are several reasons why the two-paycheck family is often the target for censure both in the church and in society as a whole.

In the first place, it must be admitted: *the two-paycheck lifestyle is controversial.* The subject of two-paycheck families—and its companion issue, the subject of working mothers—will probably always evoke strong feelings from people, no matter how common that lifestyle becomes. Jean Curtis, another author who pioneered in the subject of working mothers, writes, "People ask, 'What do you think about *it?*' 'Do you think *it*'s a good thing?' By implication, they suggest that it's a controversial topic, a situation about which one needs to have an opinion. You're either for or against working mothers in much the same way you're either for or against the use of nuclear energy."[2]

Furthermore, although two-paycheck families existed years before the women's movement picked up steam in the late 1960s, the feminist movement has tended to bring the situation into sharper focus by raising related issues such as ending discrimination against women in the labor force. For this reason, the two-paycheck lifestyle issue tends to run afoul of those who oppose the feminist movement for whatever reason. In Curtis's words, "Working mothers are now often suspected of radicalism as well as mere neglect."[3]

## Some People Are Frightened

Some people are frightened of the two-paycheck lifestyle because they fear that the institution of marriage will founder and families will fall apart as more and more women leave behind their aprons and take up their briefcases. Even some movies have picked up on this theme: a wife returns to work, becomes enthralled by her new lifestyle, and then takes off for some sort of new "freedom"—leaving behind a bewildered husband and crying children. Such stories are not supported by statistics; according to Barbara Kaye Greenleaf, a review from the American Academy of Pediatrics journal indicates that the divorce rate is no higher in two-paycheck families than it is in families where the woman is not employed outside the home.[4] But stories like that make good drama, and we suspect they are one reason why the old adage, "Woman's place is in the home—barefoot and pregnant" dies so hard. Greenleaf expresses shock that "a nation that has been so quick to accept the automobile, the TV set, and the computer" is "so reluctant to accept the working mother."[5] We tend to agree with her.

Men who become involved in professional friction and on-the-job struggles for equality with female coworkers have been known to perpetuate these attitudes because they have difficulty accepting that a woman might have the same professional ambitions as her husband, or because they feel their own jobs threatened. I've known a few men, moreover, who blame their ex-wives' careers for their divorces. On closer examination, however, I've always discovered a number of other underlying issues that probably would have broken up the marriage sooner or later anyway. It certainly evokes more sympathy to blame a marital failure on a wife's career than to accept responsibility for poor communication, abusive behavior, or another of the factors that commonly contribute to a divorce.

## A Threat and a Reminder

Another reason the two-paycheck marriage often receives criticism is that other people may view it as a threat. Some women see the dual-career family as an unpleasant reminder that they, too, could be doing something different with their lives. This may be especially true of women who slaved to get college degrees and are now spending most of their time with children and with housekeeping. They may feel guilty that their education is not being exercised more fully at the moment. "Many women who have chosen not to work, at least while their children are young, feel 'the libber's eye' on them," writes Jean Curtis. " 'I can't stand to go to a party and have somebody ask me what I do,' said one woman who had worked for seven years as a teacher before quitting to have her baby. 'If I tell them I'm a housewife or a mother, I feel oddly defensive. Like I want to tell them that I'm not just goofing off. That I'm just as bright and interesting as they are.' "[6]

Of course, not all full-time homemakers respond this way. Many are thoroughly comfortable with devoting the current chapter of their lives to working at home, and they regard working women with equanimity—simply as folks who have made a different choice from theirs. But for others not so sure of themselves, another woman's return to the work force after a stint as a homemaker can only magnify this insecurity. And being around a working husband and wife who carry off their two-paycheck lifestyle successfully may bring to the surface the unconscious fears of couples who have not resolved their own conflicts on the issue of home and career.

Kay recalls attending a local sorority alumnae function where almost all the women were homemakers. In the midst of the party, one woman came rushing in, grabbed the shoulders of a friend, and proclaimed excitedly, "You won't believe it—I got a job!" The friend's face turned a chalky white. Instead of rushing to congratulate the newly employed woman on her good fortune, the other women in the room were frozenly silent. "It was almost as though they feared that because one of their in-group had gone to work, the rest of them would instantly be forced to join the ranks of the employed, too," Kay later observed.

Psychologists have long pointed out that often people who criticize others severely are actually fighting something they fear inside themselves. Being aware that criticism may represent a deeper anxiety on the critic's part can help the two-paycheck couple to keep perspective, and to be gentle with antagonists. Such self-appointed judges may need help, love, and prayers more than they do righteous indignation and anger.

A story I heard in my childhood seems appropriate in this context. A poor farmer once set out on his donkey to take his goods to market. Someone who saw him criticized the man for overburdening the animal. So the man got off and walked, but left the goods on the donkey. A short distance later, someone else criticized the man for loading the donkey down with so much merchandise. So the man removed the goods and placed them on his own back. Then someone chastised the man for leading the poor donkey through the mud. So the man carried the donkey on his shoulders. The story ends with someone ribbing the man for being such a fool.

There will never be a time—at least in the foreseeable future—when the two-paycheck lifestyle will be warmheartedly and thoroughly embraced by everyone. Like the man on the donkey, the person who tries to please everyone will end up pleasing no one—including himself—and will be only heaping on himself much useless frustration.

## Churches Are Not Immune

In earlier chapters, we mentioned our surprise, hurt, and disappointment that church people were the primary critics of our decision to become a two-paycheck family. Somehow, we naïvely expected fellow churchgoers to be automatically compassionate, understanding, loving, and kind. The open criticism and lack of support we felt would have stung much less had these people been neighbors, coworkers, fellow carpoolers—anyone except friends in a church setting. The fact that we received such a negative response at church and such encouragement and help at work and in our neighborhood made the situation seem much worse. There was something totally inconsistent about that turn of events. We've always wanted to think of our church friends as our closest allies.

In our expectations, however, we were overlooking one important fact: church folks are like any other group made up of mere mortals; they have the same kinds of biases and weaknesses that plague any other human beings. As a religion editor on a secular newspaper, I earn my living working with church people from all denominations. Many I encounter are wonderful human beings—a joy to be around most of the time. But they are also capable of becoming grouchy and angry—even of throwing temper tantrums. Sometimes their purposes can be purely self-serving or less than honorable.

In the words of a familiar bumper sticker, "Christians aren't perfect, just forgiven." Two-paycheck families can't expect their churches to be havens of immunity from criticism, because churches are formed and operated by imperfect human beings who are striving to be better but have a long way to go. Censure of the two-paycheck lifestyle can occur as easily in a church environment as it can in a PTA group, an extended family, a civic club, or a babysitting co-op. Any time two or three are gathered together—for whatever purpose, even a missionary project—there is apt to be gossip and judgmental talk about others.

Furthermore, churches often lend themselves to being hotbeds of criticism over the two-paycheck lifestyle because they often view themselves as the protectors of traditional family values and patterns. In churches, the family unit gets a more thorough inspection than it does in a work environment or at a meeting of the Kiwanis Club. The time-honored expression, "The family that prays together, stays together," symbolizes the high value churches place on stable family units. And many churches, like much of society in general, seem to have a difficult time defining the family unit as anything other than the "Dad at work, Mom at home with the kids" model.

Churches tend to be bastions of conservative social values and forms. For this reason, when a family's lifestyle doesn't fall into the usual mold, it is far more likely to be noticed and criticized in a church setting than it would be, say, at the parent booster club for Junior's softball team or at the local garden club. In Chapter 3 we discussed some of the theological arguments for and against the two-paycheck lifestyle, and showed that much criticism of this type is culturally rather than biblically based. The same could be written about church reactions to almost any type of new or different lifestyle today.

So don't set yourself up for disappointment by expecting everyone at church to understand your needs as a two-paycheck family, especially if working couples are in the minority in your congregation. Many people will try to tune in, but others won't. It is smart to decide in advance how you will respond to those who won't tolerate or accept the way you live.

## Jesus: An Early Maverick

Surely no one in history had a lifestyle more subject to public censure than did Jesus. At every turn, he seemed to encounter someone or some group that misunderstood or disagreed with what he was teaching. Instead of running with the "temple crowd," as many expected him to do, Jesus spent his time with social outcasts, such as tax gatherers, harlots, and the demon-possessed. On one occasion, as reported in Mark 3:31–35, Jesus was even accused of ignoring his own family—his mother and brothers—at the expense of others who needed him more urgently. Most of his critics were good, temple-going folk who probably meant well by their regular criticism of Jesus' ministry and teachings. The Gospels are filled with illustrations of where Jesus kept his cool and disarmed his beraters.

For example, in the twelfth chapter of Matthew, Jesus was severely chastised by the Pharisees for allowing his disciples to pluck and eat ears of grain on the Sabbath. Jesus did not wince in the face of this criticism. Instead, he answered them directly and was not intimidated by them. Jesus said to the Pharisees, "Have you not read what David did, when he was hungry, and those who were with him: how he entered the house of God and ate the bread of the Presence, which it was not lawful for him to eat nor for those who were with him, but only for the priests? Or have you not read in the law how on the sabbath the priests in the temple profane the sabbath, and are guiltless? I tell you, something greater than the temple is here. And if you had known what this means, 'I desire mercy, and not sacrifice,' you would not have condemned the guiltless. For the son of man is lord of the sabbath" (vv. 3–8).

There is nothing indirect or weak-kneed about this statement of Jesus' to the Pharisees. He knew they were wrong, and he told them so. One gets the impression from reading these verses that if Jesus had it to do over again, he would have handled the grain-plucking incident no differently.

Another time, Jesus' critics tried to entrap him. In Matthew 22:17, the Pharisees asked Jesus, "Is it lawful to pay taxes to Caesar, or not?" Then Jesus made his famous response: "Render therefore to Caesar the things that are Caesar's, and to God the things that are God's" (v. 21). When Jesus' critics heard his answer, "They marveled; and they left him and went away" (v. 22).

I like to think of Jesus as a man who knew what he wanted and was not disturbed by his detractors. Jesus was in charge of his own life. He yielded only to the will of his father in heaven. He did not lay himself open to entrapment or make himself vulnerable by his answers to his protagonists—except when that was his intent. Sometimes he used parables and allegory, and often he answered questions with questions. On occasion, such as during his final trials before the ranking officials, Jesus even refused to answer, and turned the question back on his accusers. But at other points, he said, "If any man has ears to hear, let him hear" (Mark 4:23), by which he meant that listeners who really wanted to understand the truth of his message would do so, regardless of whether his critics did or not.

Jesus did not change his lifestyle or alter his earthly mission just because those around him—even his closest friends, the disciples—did not always agree with him or understand him. In fact, Jesus did not really expect even those who may have known him well to tune in with him 100 percent, as evidenced by his statement in Mark 6:4: "A prophet is not without honor, except in his own country, and among his own kin, and in his own house." Jesus knew that his task would not be easy, because it deviated from the norm. But he did not allow his critics to rule over him. He was secure. He knew his purpose in life, and—even in death—he pursued it boldly.

Jesus is a good model for two-paycheck families who face criticism in church. He was neither rude nor hostile to his critics. He was straightforward in his responses but unmoved by the substance of the charges. We certainly should follow his example.

## The Yellow Rain Slicker Theory

Kay has learned her own special technique for dealing with unwanted criticism. It involves the use of mental imagery. "Envision yourself wearing a child's yellow rain slicker," she said. "Pretend first that you are standing in the rain. Watch the raindrops falling and hitting the yellow vinyl or rubber. First, you see the raindrops bead up on the surface and then roll off, while you still feel dry and unviolated inside. When someone is berating you about your lifestyle, just imagine yourself putting on your yellow raincoat and watch the words and barbs of criticism roll off in the same way the raindrops roll off the coat. The raincoat represents your self-esteem. If you think well of yourself, the raindrops of social disapproval will not bother you."

We also like to remember this definition of judgment that we read long ago but have since forgotten the source for: "Judgment is merely someone saying, 'I don't understand what you are doing and why you are doing it.'" Give your critics that right not to understand. Instead of allowing someone's critical barbs to shut a door in a relationship, allow them to be a vehicle for opening a window. Look on that criticism as an opportunity to let others understand you better. Perhaps a fresh glimpse of the two-paycheck lifestyle as modeled by you will cause your critics to be more tolerant in the future or maybe even join the ranks.

## The Inspirations of Others

In no other area were we inspired by the couples we interviewed as when they discussed how they respond to criticism. Although not every couple had experienced direct or even indirect censure from fellow churchgoers, all had very clear-cut ideas about how they would deal with criticism should it ever arise. Without exception, those who seemed to pull off the two-paycheck lifestyle most effectively were those who were thoroughly committed to their decision and who discounted the opinions of others. They wore their yellow rainslickers confidently. They said that, even if they faced stern opposition from other church members, they would ignore it and do what they felt was best for themselves and their families.

An example of this attitude was the self-assured response of journalist Madeleine Hamm, a Methodist, who said, "If I feel strongly about what I am doing, I wonder what is wrong with the other person who tries to cut me down. If you're secure, it's the best insurance policy."

Presbyterians Jean and Charlie Storm were another couple who exuded confidence about their way of life. "I don't care at all what the masses think of me," said Jean. "I care only for what people I look up to think." Jean said she receives "so many positive strokes" in her work that the opinions of others are "immaterial."

Lutherans Carol and Ted Dinkins are old pros at fielding attacks on their unconventional choices. "There's been very little in our lives that someone might not criticize," said Carol. The Dinkins married while they were still in undergraduate school; Carol became pregnant while in law school but continued her studies. She joined a major law firm when their daughters were still preschoolers, and now she commutes on the plane weekly from their home in Texas to her full-time job in the nation's capital, leaving her children in the care of Ted and a governess.

"Most people know me well enough to know that we must have something figured out," said Carol. Should negative remarks arise, she said, "I would tell them I appreciate how they feel. I'd tell them I appreciate that they understand it isn't easy to do the kinds of things that we do, but I don't think there is anyone who can make the decision

quite like we can, because we're the only ones who have
to live with it."

Carol's lawyer-husband Ted offered this answer: "I'd tell
them I appreciate their interest. If they weren't concerned
about us, they would not have expressed an opinion."

## Confront with Facts

Several couples we interviewed said they simply rely on
the facts when confronted with criticism about being a two-
paycheck family.

Although they can't recite any specific instances in which
their lifestyle has come under attack in their Disciples of
Christ congregation, Dana and Red Gordon said they are
geared up to handle unkind remarks about placing their
young daughter, Sara, in day care. "Sara is better off socially
than kids who stay home all the time," said Red. "It's the
best socializing experience she could have."

Linda and John Ahsmann said they know what they
would answer if anyone at their Methodist church ever
wished to do battle with them about being a working couple
with children: "I'd say, 'I'm sorry you feel that way, but
the kids are well taken care of; I maintain my home the
way I like and enjoy my career,' " said Linda.

When friends in her small-town Baptist church jumped
Donna Oates for returning to work as a teacher after her
son was born, she pointed out that these same women "leave
their children for many hours a day in the church nursery
to go to Baptist Young Women, Bible study, Sunday school
luncheons and other church social activities." She said she
saw no difference in leaving her son with a sitter so she
could go to work to help support the family and these
women "parking" their children to free themselves for social
activities many hours a day.

Donna also said she found it best to be truthful about
why their family needed an extra income. "I told them
that my husband Bob went back to graduate school and

that we needed the money," she said. She believes that an honest explanation helped stem the tide of criticism, because no one could dispute the facts.

## A Direct Blessing from God?

Many of Royce Smith's Baptist church friends were shocked to learn that she was taking a job outside the home after being a full-time mother to her two daughters. "We had always put our kids first, and they [church friends] felt that meant we might not be doing that now," said Royce. Although no one attacked her directly, Royce said she experienced "little probing questions" like "Who's keeping the kids?" and "How do you know the sitter is good?" and dogmatic statements like, "Well, I'm certainly not ever going to work," when she announced her new arrangement.

When confronted, the Smiths consistently told their friends they saw Royce's job as "a direct blessing from God," because they had prayed diligently that the right type of work would come available. "We pray about everything," said her husband Skip. "We prayed about every aspect of her going back to work." The Smiths said they felt that if God had not intended for Royce to take an outside job, he would have put roadblocks in Royce's path. Instead, every problem they expected to encounter during the switch from being a one-paycheck family worked out smoothly. In fact, every obstacle vanished from in front of them in such a way that the Smiths could only conclude that God willed Royce to work. That's exactly what they tell friends who approach them with critical comments to offer.

Donna and Bob Porter said they would approach criticism in a similar fashion if anyone at their Free Methodist Church decided to attack their two-paycheck lifestyle or her leaving toddler son David in a day-care center during the day. "I just have to trust that God sent David to us to raise and

we have faith to believe that God is taking care of him,"
said Donna, a teacher. She said the fact that David stays
in a church-run rather than a commercial day-care center
may make others more apt to approve. Donna also said,
"I feel like God put me there [in her school situation]. It's
not a job; it's a ministry." Such an attitude likely goes a
long way to deter her critics.

## Choosing the Right Support Systems

Lawyers Linda and Eric King said they meet with disapproval of their two-paycheck lifestyle on almost every turn
in their Church of Christ congregation. "Many people, including our preacher, still believe woman's place is in the
home," said Linda. "We have had sermons intimating this,
along with paeans to the housewife. Usually the criticism
from individuals is polite and indirect, such as 'Maybe some
women can be a good mother and wife and have a career,
but I know I certainly can't be,' which translates to, 'And
we don't think you can do it either.'" The Kings said they
long ago decided to ignore criticism rather than answer it
directly. "Occasionally we answer something head-on, but
seldom does it seem useful," said Linda.

The Kings said they learned over the years the importance
of choosing and cultivating a strong support group to help
them cope with their two-paycheck lifestyle. They regularly
share fellowship with six other two-paycheck couples. "It
is extremely helpful to get together and compare notes and
gripes and whine around together. There's an honesty
among such gatherings of friends that can't be found elsewhere," said Linda. Furthermore, she said, "we have a
throng of relatives close by who not only approve and affirm
us, but who offer help in a practical sense—occasional babysitting, errand-swapping and so forth."

Donna Oates said she originally felt sorry for herself because her teaching job kept her from spending as much
time as she had previously done with her church friends,

who were all full-time homemakers. Eventually, however, she made a new set of friends in the working world and "put the past behind me." Now, some five years later, Donna takes pride in pointing out that most of the women who criticized her lifestyle switch have now taken outside jobs themselves. Perhaps they criticized her initially because they were fighting what they saw as the inevitable for their own lives. "These things have a way of working themselves out," said Donna.

Choosing her friends very carefully during the time period when she was resuming her teaching career after taking time off to have a baby probably helped Ann Sullivan escape direct criticism at her Baptist church. Ann said that during those days she deliberately made it a point not to go around people whom she knew would disapprove, and sought out people whom she knew would understand and sympathize with the changes occurring in their family.

Ann also said she avoided criticism because "I was already in a teaching position in church when I went back to work and not a member of a Sunday school class planning those little luncheons."

Discretion also seemed to pay off for Lutheran Janet Zaozirny. "I simply didn't go around the church talking about it [the fact that her daughter was in day care while she worked]" said Janet, a counselor. Her husband Clarence said that if criticism ever came his way, "I'd just consider the source."

## Other Approaches

Teacher Sandra Lengefeld had a slightly different approach which she said was successful regarding possible criticism of their two-paycheck lifestyle. "I usually agree with them," she said. "My friends know that if I had my choice, I'd probably stay home." Because of this, Sandra said her friends in her Baptist church who might be tempted to criticize know they would not find Sandra the least bit phased by their comments. She'd agree with them. And sometimes there is no better way to disarm a critic than to concur with all he or she says and then go right on living and doing exactly how you feel you must!

However, Catholic Beverly Herbert used just the opposite approach in her church when she heard unkind remarks about her being a part of a working couple team. Because two-paycheck couples are rapidly becoming a dominant lifestyle in society, "I simply reflect that most people live the same way I do, and that the person doing the criticizing is not facing up to this particular reality of life," said Beverly, who works in public relations.

At their Episcopal church, which is mostly black with a strong minority of whites, Lou and James Barron said they've encountered no criticism and do not expect any. "Black women have always combined careers and motherhood," said James. He said it would be a rarity for a black person to even attempt to criticize the two-paycheck family because of the historical perspective. And the white members of the Barrons' Episcopal church tend to be socially liberal, so they would not likely criticize a working couple either, he said.

## Suffering in Silence

Criticism from friends at their Church of Christ centered around charges of "materialism" when Vicki Black took a job outside the home. Vicki said she went back to work after a long stint home with their two daughters because Mike's income as a salesman had suffered a setback and Vicki was trying to make up for the loss.

Vicki's first employment was as a receptionist at their church. That stirred no ill-will, because friends considered that working on the church staff was doing the "Lord's work." But trouble set in when Vicki left the church position and took a more lucrative job as a receptionist at a large downtown bank. Even though the increase in salary was still not enough to offset Mike's lost income, it raised the ire of some church friends. When Vicki told their minister that she was quitting her church job, his response was, "Some people say you've become too materialistic." That remark stung to the core, she said. Vicki said she found the dig especially hard to stomach because much of her salary was earmarked to pay off earlier pledges she and Mike had made to the church's building fund back in the days when Mike's salary was higher.

Things got even stickier for the Blacks when they traded in their aging 1966-model automobile for a sporty new car. On top of the job switch, the new car set even more tongues to wagging about the Blacks' alleged materialism. "Even our daughters began hearing remarks at church," said Vicki. "It got to where they were almost afraid to show up at church with new clothes on." Older women in the congregation also became a problem for the Blacks. "They kept asking me, 'When are you going to quit work?' " recalled Vicki. "They apparently assumed that the new lifestyle was only temporary. Others whom I'm sure were well-meaning would tell me, 'Please don't work too hard.' " To Vicki's ears, such remarks also sounded like criticism.

At the time we interviewed the Blacks, who probably bore more battle scars than did all the other couples combined from trying to mix a two-paycheck lifestyle with an active church life, they were still searching for a positive approach to deal with the criticism. Until they could devise a better way, their technique seemed to be "suffering in silence." Although hurt by the church's response, the Blacks obviously had chosen to cope by keeping stiff upper lips. However, if the Blacks allowed their experience to interfere with church activities or with their dedication, they were keeping it well hidden. We had to rush to complete our interview with them so they could dash off to church for the Sunday evening service.

## Some Tips for Handling Criticism

A friend who was about to take a job as a high school home economics teacher recently sought Kay's advice about how to handle hostile comments from friends. Besides sharing what we learned from interviewing two-paycheck families for this book, Kay offered this friend these pointers which she gleaned from personal experiences:

(1) *Categorize your critics.* Some will be people whose opinions don't matter; others may be people you highly respect. If the latter is true, don't be so defensive about your lifestyle that you overlook some good advice. No one person has all the answers, and it is possible that a trusted friend could shed some helpful light on your situation.

(2) *Count your blessings.* Make a list of how many people in the past month, for example, have said something affirming, have complimented your work, have said they admire you. Does one of those people happen to be your mother or father? If so, count that person at least three times on your list. It's a boon to have someone of an older generation as part of your support group. Ditto goes for one of your children. If your own offspring are in your corner, you've got it made.

(3) *Don't be afraid to seek out encouragement; you don't always have to wait for it to come your way.* If the barbs about your lifestyle are getting you down, deliberately seek out someone—maybe another member of a two-paycheck family—whom you know understands, and tell them you sorely need a kind word or two. One friend who recently returned to work told about finding a "prayer partner," another teacher at her school. The two of them agreed to pray for each other as they encountered struggles in their efforts to combine home and work. But be realistic about whom you ask for support. Don't ask someone who is convinced women belong at home in the kitchen to give you reassurances about your lifestyle!

(4) *Keep your cool.* Flying off the handle at someone's

thoughtless comment about your lifestyle can only hurt and not help your cause. It can prove just what your critic suspects—that members of a two-paycheck family are frazzled, at their wits' end, and perpetually sitting on a powder keg. Giving an unruffled answer to a critic will go miles toward proving that you're in control.

(5) *Keep a sense of humor and don't take yourself too seriously.* For example, when the man at the Wednesday night supper table singled out Matthew's roughhousing for comment, our automatic response might have been to say, "How dare you?" But fortunately I had enough foresight to reply, "Well, he simply takes after his boisterous parents." The man left the table with a smile on his face. Another answer from us might have closed the door to a potential friendship.

(6) *Don't project.* Many times people who comment on your lifestyle may be just curious, toying with becoming a two-paycheck family themselves or merely making small talk. Try to accept comments you hear at their face value and don't read hostility into them unless it's present beyond a shadow of a doubt. Be aware of your own guilt feelings and learn to express them in healthy ways, so you won't project them onto innocent people.

(7) *If others' criticism causes you to have doubts, don't worry.* Everyone at some point doubts the wisdom of his actions. Doubts can sometimes be creative because they stimulate the thinking process and can keep you from getting into a mental rut or having tunnel vision. Anytime you dare to do something different, you can't possibly know the outcome. And if things don't work out, be assured that that's OK, too. If you feel good about yourself, you'll know you can find alternatives regardless.

(8) *The Bible verse says it all:* "Bless those who curse you, pray for those who mistreat you" (Luke 6:28, NAS). If you feel you've been wronged, be forgiving. It not only helps those who have wronged you—it helps you, too!

# 8. Juggling Your Act

A friend who recently started working at a part-time job arrived at church one Wednesday evening looking understandably weary. Someone asked her if her new job was difficult. "My job is easy," she replied. "The work starts when I get home."

In two sentences, she summarized one of the biggest problems of the two-paycheck lifestyle. The on-the-job demands of two careers are usually a piece of cake compared to the endless array of household duties that hang like a dark cloud over working couples when the five o'clock whistle blows. Unless the couple is wealthy and can afford around-the-clock paid help, they face a staggering number of tasks to accomplish during their limited home hours. Lawns need to be mowed. Children need time. Clothes need to be bought, mended, washed, ironed, or taken to the cleaners. Friendships need to be cultivated. The marriage needs attention.

The oft-heard comment from two-paycheck couples, "What we *both* need is a wife at home during the day," is no laughing matter. We agree with Barbara Kaye Greenleaf's description: "What really separates the working mother from the rest of the world is time. You probably have less of it in which to do more things for more people than [do] most of the other men, women, and children on this earth."[1]

When one marriage partner is home during the day, tasks are apportioned over a twelve-to-fourteen hour period. Even if she is doing church or civic work, taking college courses or playing bridge, there is usually time to take care of basic household chores. But when both spouses work outside the home, they often feel like race horses covering a vast track in a limited time stretch, as they try to compensate for the absent full-time homemaker in their lives.

A two-paycheck husband and wife can become so swallowed up by the mundane tasks of keeping the household running that they have no time for church—much less for other spiritual replenishment, such as daily devotions, family worship, personal meditation. Weekends especially are prime "catch-up time" for these necessary deeds, and some people simply write church completely off the agenda in order to keep the home fires burning.

Recently several excellent books on time management have been published to help the working couple best utilize their home hours. We've already referred to two of them: *Working Mothers* by Jean Curtis and *Help: A Handbook for Working Mothers* by Barbara Kaye Greenleaf. Two others we like are *Working Couples* by Hilary Ryglewicz and Pat Koch Thaler and *Double Duties* by Cynthia Sterling Pincus.[2] Each book offers a different perspective on how a family can organize itself, and in this chapter we've drawn from some of these ideas. We highly recommend that any two-paycheck family read at least one book for its practical suggestions on home management.

However, we've found the best source of tips to be our interviewees—the two-paycheck families who have become pros at staying active in church in addition to carrying out their home and work responsibilities. They shared their tricks for juggling all the aspects of their complex lives. Besides giving techniques for doing the "dirty work" at home, they told of some ingenious ways to simplify churchgoing, so that in the crush of activities, church does not get erased from the list of "things to do."

## Five Basic Trends

As we gleaned ideas from other couples about how they manage, we detected several basic principles which seemed to stand out:

(1) *Each family is unique.* No two families have exactly the same mix of needs, personalities, talents, situations, or schedules, so there is no one time management solution for all families. In our twelve years as a two-paycheck family, we have tried a variety of arrangements, which seemed to change each time there was a shift in our lifestyle, such as a new job, a move to a new house, or a new baby. Just about the time we would get one system down pat, it seemed we were having to reshuffle it or to abandon it in favor of another.

The couples we interviewed varied greatly in the amount of organizing and planning they do to keep things running smoothly. One of the differences was most apparent in our discussions about list-making and calendars. Linda and Larry Calvert said their household calendar was a major factor in the success of their lifestyle. They each keep personal calendars at work, and bring those home periodically to copy appointments on the master schedule. Martha Haun said she is an inveterate list-maker. "Sometimes I get up at 2:00 A.M. to make lists," she said. Linda and Eric King give credit to the motto of their law firm—"Organization and Preparation"—for the success of their lifestyle at home, too. "We make lists, keep a calendar on which we and the children note all obligations, activities and so forth," said Linda. In our house, a small chalkboard hangs by the door where we leave for work every morning. Items written on it jiggle our memories if we've forgotten something we're supposed to do that day. On the other hand, Linda and John Ahsmann reject the whole idea of list-making. John, who is in the interior decorating business, said he has seen many lists posted inside cabinet doors of many homes. "I always note that nothing on the lists is ever done," he said.

(2) *There's no such thing as his-and-her chores.* Attempting to hold onto traditional roles while living as a working couple simply did not wash in these households. We found very few women who were stuck in the "superwoman" or martyr role of trying to hold down a job without sharing the demands of the household. Although the amount of housework the husbands took care of varied, we found that each family basically operated on an egalitarian concept. Husbands felt free to iron their own shirts and their wives' blouses. Wives had no qualms about toting garbage and repairing leaky faucets.

Linda and John Ahsmann said their pet phrase is "Whoever gets there first does it." At their home, this motto applies to fixing dinner, changing sheets, folding laundry— whatever the current need of the moment seems to be. Beverly Hebert said, "We all have our usual chores, but sometimes the one who has the most time and energy at a particular hour is the one who gets the groceries or cleans the kitchen or takes a child to piano practice."

Judy and Jim Dougherty have a similar attitude toward chores. They take turns cooking: he one night and she the next. They swap out picking up the children after work. They divide yard duties: Jim likes to mow; Judy works the flower beds. Jean and Charlie Storm sort out chores based on what's best suited for each and what is least distasteful. Charlie vacuums and washes windows "because he has longer arms," said Jean. "He also likes to bake bread."

(3) *Setting priorities is crucial.* "The level of tolerance for a life in which some things never get done is probably a working couple's most valuable asset," write Hilary Ryglewicz and Pat Koch Thaler.[3] Couples we interviewed seemed to be aware of their own limitations and knew how quickly they could exhaust themselves by trying to cram too much into a day or a week. These families had decided what basics were necessary for their own peace of mind and well-being, and had put the other chores in a "Who cares?" category.

For example, Bob Lobaugh said, "We had to learn to say no to things like tennis and other luxuries and to do the minimum of activities just to get by."

At our house, Kay would rather spend the "unwind" hour before she goes to bed stitching on needlepoint than she would manicuring her nails. Because of this trade-off, she's accepted the fact that having a good manicure may be a semi-annual event and a luxury for her at the most.

For me, having well-manicured lawns and shrubs are worth sacrificing at least three hours every Saturday morning, while other people, like John Ahsmann, have chosen the minimal yard maintenance of a condominium in order to have free time Saturday.

For the couples we interviewed, the specific choices they made were not as important as the fact that those choices represented consciously set goals and priorities. Most couples knew exactly what they wanted out of life and knew what they were sacrificing to obtain it.

(4) *The two-paycheck lifestyle requires commitment.* In home management, more than in any other area we found, the key to successfully managing a two-paycheck lifestyle was believing in it! No matter how firm their agreement to share household tasks, couples did not last long in their agreement if they secretly expected the new arrangement to fail. Faith that the system would work seemed to be the glue that kept both spouses committed to a smoothly running home. As Linda Calvert put it, "What it really boils down to is that you have to know beyond a shadow of a doubt that it can be done."

We once knew a husband and wife who gave only lip-service to being a two-paycheck family. Although they both drafted a contract for dividing up chores, secretly neither of them gave the new system a very good chance of succeeding. Slowly, the husband began drifting away from his domestic tasks, because he never really embraced the idea of his wife's working. Their less-than-full commitment drove the first nail in the coffin for their two-paycheck lifestyle. To no one's surprise, the wife quit work after the first year.

(5) *Teamwork works.* A strong sense of group effort is needed to make a two-paycheck lifestyle work—and this includes the use of "kid power" in households with children. Two-paycheck families have learned that everyone must pitch in, with no free ride for anybody. In fact, children in homes where both parents work seem to carry their own weight to a much greater extent than those we know whose mothers are full-time homemakers.

Mary Frances and Mark Henry told us, "We pay our teen-age boys to do the house chores. Anything we would pay someone else to do, we now pay them." Janet Zaozirny said, "The children do such things as change the sheets on their beds." Our son, Matthew, recently bought his first bicycle with money he earned over an eight-month period by sweeping the patio, carrying out plants to be watered, mopping floors, sweeping sidewalks, and performing other household duties that fell outside the realm of his usual responsibilities like straightening his room and setting the table.

Linda Ahsmann made this insightful comment about tapping the housecleaning talents of her children: "If you do give them tasks to do, you must accept the way it is done. You shouldn't rush in and redo it." Respecting children's limitations seemed to be a key in the Ahsmann family for accomplishing chores.

Authors Ryglewicz and Thaler write, "[Having the kids pitch in] doesn't mean that everything automatically runs smoothly or that getting work done doesn't involve some argument and conflict. But at least, when both parents work, there is some shift in expectations: the unspoken feelings that 'Mom can do it; after all, that's what she's there for' is replaced, to some extent, by the recognition that, 'If I don't do it, who will?' "[4]

There is another very definite advantage to having children participate in the running of a household. When a boy or girl learns to pitch in and get necessary chores done, he or she learns some good work habits that will be hard to forget in later years, when that son or daughter is a young adult!

## So How Can It Be Done?

My maternal grandparents were a working couple, even though they lived in another era. Their work, however, all went on at the same general location—he was a farmer, and she was a farmer's wife. These forebears died before I was born, at what we now consider retirement age, but my memory is filled with stories I have heard about how my grandmother ran her home with nine children. Their basement was packed with huge vats of homemade grape jelly, and cellar walls were lined with myriad jars of home-canned vegetables, fruits, and meats. There was even a sweet potato house out back.

Although technology has intervened to make life easier for us, with appliances like vacuum cleaners, dishwashers, freezers, and garbage disposals, and nearby grocery stores with a stock of fresh, frozen, and canned goods, running a home is still no simple task. Modern conveniences may have freed women from their domestic duties and helped make it easier for women in the business and professional world, but those modern conveniences don't do everything for us. So how does the nitty gritty all get done in a two-paycheck family?

Ann Sullivan said her first word of advice to any woman considering taking an outside job is "hire a maid." This, of course, is nearly everyone's dream solution. Lawyers Carol and Ted Dinkins' income level allows them outside help to simplify their two-paycheck marriage; their full-time housekeeper cleans and runs the house, and a gardener keeps the yard. At the time we visited them, the Dinkins

were attempting to hire a summertime governess to drive
their daughters to lessons and show them around Washington, D.C., where Carol works during the week.

But outside full-time help is not everyone's answer, usually for financial considerations; those we interviewed who
hired outside help were able to do so for once or twice a
week at most. But there are problems other than financial
ones that go with hiring someone to handle household
chores. Dependable help is hard to find. And many women
feel that hiring someone to do their housework is exploitive.
They often simply feel better doing it themselves!

Jean and Charlie Storm, the entrepreneur and oil company
executive, were in this category. Their combined income
was high enough that they could well afford domestic help.
But Charlie said he was "too Scotch" to spend money on
something he could do himself. Jean said she and Charlie
like to "cover all the bases ourselves." They seemed proud
that their gleaming, spotless house and well-pressed clothes
were the products of their own elbow grease.

Our personal experience with hiring outside help has not
been positive. For about eight years, a maid cleaned our
house and washed our clothes once a week. But the financial
and emotional toll was great. The constant worry of keeping
up with the maid's erratic bus schedules, temperamental
personality, and irritating personal habits were more than
we were willing to endure any longer. In the year after
we dismissed the maid, we saved enough money by doing
the work ourselves to purchase two new sofas for the den.

For us, then, and for the Storms, hiring outside help has
not been a satisfactory answer to the problems of the two-
paycheck time crunch. Other couples, like the Dinkins, have
found outside help to be a lifesaver. As with other aspects
of the two-paycheck lifestyle, whether or not to hire household help is something each couple must decide for themselves, keeping in mind their budget, priorities, and
temperaments.

## Housekeeping—The Lowest Priority

In almost every interview, working couples described a very ho-hum approach to housekeeping, and assigned it a very low priority on their lists of things to do. Since they simply aren't at home for "white glove inspections," they did not try to meet any sort of perfectionistic standards. "In the beginning, when I went back to work, we asked ourselves, 'Just how clean do we want this house to be anyway?' " said Mary Frances Henry. "It was then I discovered that I was cleaning just for my mother." She said she was setting up some artificial requirements for neatness she thought her mother would sanction. As Hilary Ryglewicz and Pat Thaler wrote, people who work "have little time to look in corners, let alone clean in them."[5]

However, almost every home we visited was extremely orderly and clean (although several couples indicated they had just tidied up especially for our interview). In fact, some of the messiest houses we've ever been in have been run by full-time homemakers who talk in glowing terms about keeping window blinds spotless and making sure that all the towels are turned the same directions in their closets.

So if housecleaning is at the bottom of the working couple's totem pole, how does it get done?

Sandra and Curtis Lengefeld benefit by the fact that Curtis is often home during weekdays because of his shift work, and is willing and able to vacuum, mop, and dust whenever necessary.

Most couples listed Saturday as their target day for housecleaning, saying they are simply too tired to attempt it on a work night. Dana Gordon said she devotes Saturday afternoon to cleaning while husband Red shops for groceries. On Sunday afternoons, then, Red babysits with daughter Sara while Dana sews so she can make most of her own clothes.

Donna Porter was partial to Friday night cleaning hours,

saying, "I never can relax then anyway after a week at work."

Others, however, described their system as thoroughly catch-as-catch-can. Barbara and Terry Myers said they had no set time for housework. "Basically, we just let it pile up until one of us can't stand it any longer, and then that person initiates the cleaning," said Barbara. And Mike Hamm commented, "Why bother to make up the bed when the dog will just mess it up during the day anyway?"

Kay and I list ourselves in the minority: we give house-keeping a slightly higher billing. We like our home to be orderly at all times, not just for company, but for our own appreciation. Although we've been accused of being slightly neurotic about a neat environment, we both agree that work days seem to go better when we leave the house with beds made, dishes washed, and toys and books picked up. When our house is disheveled, we feel disheveled. When we come home at night to orderly rooms, we feel less overwhelmed by home life in general.

Because we discovered early in our marriage that we shared a tendency to be persnickety about housecleaning, we've used several systems throughout the years, in addition to the maid we mentioned earlier. One of our most effective methods originated in a book called *Sidetracked Home Executives*,[6] by Peggy Jones and Pam Brace, which Kay stumbled upon when she reviewed the book for a newspaper story.

The system relied on a set of three-by-five index cards, on which the couple writes every household chore performed in the course of the week. Each chore is assigned to a color-coded day file in the card box. On Monday, for example, out comes the card for cleaning the upstairs bath, washing kids' clothes, and sponging out the refrigerator. When a task is completed, its card is initialed and put back into the "Monday" slot until the next week.

A similar system kept track of monthly tasks such as paying the bills and balancing the checkbook, as well as yearly jobs, such as buying a vast supply of air conditioner filters and pruning trees and rose bushes. The card file system spread chores out over a longer time span, and was designed to prevent the fatigue that occurs when all chores are crammed into one afternoon's agenda.

We monitored our file religiously and admit that it kept us well organized and on target during the six-month period we followed it. However, we eventually drifted away from the system when we began to feel we were "cleaning house every night." Kay complained that the piecemeal approach never allowed for a day when the entire house seemed clean all at the same time. Somehow a well-mopped kitchen and clean oven didn't feel like such a big accomplishment if the furniture in the adjacent den remained dusty until two nights later.

Gradually, housekeeping evolved into a Thursday night project, a system we still find suitable. Thursday was chosen because it was close to the weekend. The goal of having everything done by Saturday became a motivating factor. After a take-out meal at McDonald's or another stop along our nearby fast food strip, we spent a packed two hours tackling all the laundry, dusting, vacuuming, linen-changing, mopping, and tidying we could possibly work in. Matthew was much more compelled to pipe up, "What can I do, Mommy?", since he did not want to be excluded from projects that obviously were intended to occupy our entire Thursday evening. By bedtime, we were ready to drop, but the feeling of accomplishment was gratifying. Setting aside a block of time for housework and guarding it jealously seemed to suit our temperaments better than did any system we had tried previously.

## Marketing

Unlike dust, food is not a matter that can be swept under the rug and put off until a later date. Hunger is no respector of whether one or both of the adults in the house have full-time jobs. As long as human beings exist in a household, there must be food on the table (or arrangements made for it) three times a day. Because of their time constraints, working couples can't afford to wait until 6:00 P.M. for some inspiration about the evening meal to occur to them. So marketing must take place with considerable thought.

When we moved to Houston ten years ago, I was amazed to see a number of other men who frequented our local supermarket, not just for fill-in items, but for the full family marketing. Lists and coupons in hand, they prowled the aisles, seriously shopping for bargains and reading ingredients to get the best buys for their families. Therefore, we were not surprised when a number of husbands in our interviews said they also were actively involved with the weekly marketing.

Some couples followed rigid schemes of meal planning and food buying. "An unorganized person would be miserable trying to keep up with me at the grocery store," said Ann Sullivan. She said she makes strict lists and doesn't deviate from them, because impulse buying wastes time. "Time is my most valuable possession," she said.

At our house, we try to keep a running list all week when we discover an item is low. Even Matthew is encouraged to alert us when his supply of snack foods, such as ice cream bars, raisins, or cheese slices, is almost exhausted. Throughout the week, Kay clips recipes from the food section of the newspaper or pulls recipes from her recipe card file that she has in mind for the coming week's menus. Then when she sits down for a quiet half hour with the grocery list before going to the store, all the information she needs to add to the list is at hand. We clip and store coupons in a shoebox, which Kay or I usually leaf through before going to the store to make the purchases.

Other couples said they hang loose and try to be as flexible as possible with their food buying. "We don't do meal planning," said Jim Dougherty. He and his wife Judy "try to have as much on hand as possible so we can have a selection to choose from." Martha Haun also buys in bulk for the sake of convenience. "If I buy soup, I buy eight cans at a time," she said. "It takes the same amount of time and energy to pick up large quantities as it does to buy just one item. The babysitter says I have the best-stocked pantry anywhere." Her husband Bill is into home canning, which also helps keep their larder well supplied. Janet Zaozirny shops big every three weeks, then goes back to the grocery store periodically for the incidental items.

Most people said they deliberately choose shopping times when the stores are least crowded, to expedite purchases and reduce stress levels for the shopper. Sandra Lengefeld said she rises early on Saturday mornings and hits the store between 7:30 and 8 A.M., before the Saturday rush begins. Kay and I both enjoy this practice because we feel our concentration level is greater early on Saturday than it would be on a work night. Madeleine Hamm and Barbara Myers do their marketing on Sunday afternoons after church. Martha Haun, whose hours at the university give her some flexibility, likes to shop "in the early afternoons on weekdays when there is a low population in the stores."

Although shopping the values at the various stores no doubt saves money, most of our couples said they prefer to find one trusty supermarket where prices were reasonable overall, and to stick with it. Shopping a store you know like the back of your hand can be a time-saver because you can negotiate the aisles confidently without having to spend precious minutes hunting down products.

## Resourceful Cooking

A well-stocked pantry doesn't put food on the table. Again, our interviews show there is a trend toward more participation by the husbands in the kitchen—usually the last bastion to fall to fifty-fifty division, even in the most progressive family. Some men like Jim Dougherty split kitchen duty evenly with their wives. But most said they were willing to "lend a hand" to whip up a meal when necessary. Even men who seemed reluctant to get involved with actual meal preparation turned out to be handy with the outdoor barbecue grill. Their wives said they relied heavily on charcoaling to offset their husbands' inability or unwillingness to follow a recipe.

Anything cooked ahead of time is a boon to these two-paycheck families, who usually don't have a moment to spare once they hit the home front. Dana Gordon said she relies heavily on the freezer to make their lifestyle run smoothly. "Before I went back to work, I cooked up three weeks' worth of meals for the deep-freeze," she said. It's still a schedule she tries to stick to as often as possible.

We have also found the freezer—and the microwave oven—a distinct asset in preparing wholesome meals in minimal time. On weekday nights, a frozen casserole can be warmed in the microwave while we heat a vegetable on the stove and make a salad. By using this method, we've found we can easily have dinner on the table within fifteen minutes after we walk in the door.

Sharon and John Lawson said they use sealable plastic bags to save leftovers for easy meals later. We also try to make leftovers work for us. On weekends, even when it's not possible to cook and freeze in bulk, we at least try to cook with some foresight: roasts or briskets which will do for several meals and Sunday night casseroles which will amply supply enough for leftovers on Monday and Tuesday.

Donna Oates and a neighbor who's also a working mother have come up with an ingenious idea: once a week, each of them doubles a recipe for a dish they cook for their family; then they exchange the extra dish. "We'll either freeze it or serve it right away," said Donna. "If my family particularly likes the meal she's brought over, I'll get the recipe and try it on my own."

When there's been no advance effort and meals must be cooked on the spot, one of the best ideas we've read

comes from *Help: A Handbook for Working Mothers:* consider
thumbing through children's cookbooks for quick, non-
exotic menus. A good cookbook will offer some stripped-
down recipes that usually are nourishing and involve only
a few steps in preparation.[7]

Several people asserted that the non-exotic was what they
really prefer anyway. Mike Hamm commented: "If it takes
more than five minutes to cook, it's not worth eating." He
said he and wife Madeleine "consider being together more
important than eating fancy foods."

Kay and I will settle for bare-bones menus like hot dogs
or tunafish salad on weeknights, as long as these foods
are accompanied by vegetables from the freezer, and as
long as we've had at least one elaborate meal on our days
off. At least one night during the weekend, Kay tries to
experiment with new recipes and prepare something akin
to a gourmet meal, "just because it does my ego good. I
like to prove to myself I can do it." The rest of the week,
she's content to open cans or pop food out of the freezer.

Eating out routinely also seemed to go hand in hand with
being a two-paycheck family, and no one seemed to apolo-
gize for their regular fare of non-homecooked food. As a
matter of fact, Dana and Red Gordon said eating out is
"an absolute essential" to making their working-couple
lifestyle work. Donna and Bob Porter said they visit a cafeteria once a week. Sandra and Curtis Lengefeld said their
favorite fast-food stop is Kentucky Fried Chicken, especially on Sundays. McDonalds and a take-out Mexican restaurant, which loads its tacos and tostadas down with an
ample helping of tomatoes, lettuce, and cheese to assuage
the conscience, are our favorite "quickie" haunts.

Vicki and Mike Black offered a different twist to the
idea of eating out regularly. Instead of rushing around each
weekday evening fixing brown bag lunches for the next
day, both Vicki and Mike dine out on their lunch breaks
and try to make their noon meal their "big meal" for the
day—replete with vegetables, fiber, and essential nutrients.

They encourage their daughters to do likewise in the school cafeteria. Then they can scrimp on dinner to make things go more smoothly at night.

## Time for The Children

Not allowing one's children to become the "stepchildren" of a two-paycheck lifestyle is a true challenge. Working couples who are parents often feel plagued with the question, "How can I squeeze more time into my day to get to know my child better?" Such couples find they must deliberately seize every opportunity for intimate contact with their children, or they miss out on good parenting altogether.

Ann and Doug Sullivan said their planning started when they deliberately limited their family size to one child because they saw a large family as totally incompatible with a two-paycheck lifestyle. "I never saw how I could keep my head above water and have two kids," said Ann.

Linda and Eric King, who have to spread their attentions among three offspring, schedule Fridays as "family night" at their house. "We make a conscious effort to reserve the night, without resentment," said Linda. "We may go swimming or bowling or to the show. Or we stay home and play dominos or games or watch TV and have popcorn or pizza. We try to really listen to what they [the children] have to say. Both our friends and the kids' friends know about our family night, so we don't have as many invitations to do other things on Fridays as we used to."

Martha and Bill Haun said they've developed an almost automatic "no" to outside social invitations so they can stay home with their three daughters. "We'd just rather be home with our kids at night," said Bill. "Our social life is our family."

One of our most successful quality times as a family is a part of the day most working couples dread—the commute to work. Because Matthew's school is on the way to our office—a total trip of one hour on the freeway—we have a long stretch of uninterrupted time to spend "connecting" with him and with each other. In the closed-in space of the car, we are able to sing, read stories, play guessing games, or talk about what's happened to each of us during the day. We have trouble relating to people who talk about "a long, boring drive to and from work," since our family time in the car makes us almost oblivious to the congested freeway.

Even on the days we've had to carpool and to transport other kids to school, we've tried not to count our commuting time as a loss. Just listening to how Matthew interacts with his peers—his conversations about school activities and teachers—gives us more insight into what goes on during the hours he's away from us. And to combat the age-old problem of encountering dead silence when we ask a child, "What did you do at school today?" we begin conversations by telling about what we have done at work—who we had lunch with, where we went on interviews, and even troubling experiences we have had, like disagreements with colleagues. As a result of what we share, Matthew has become much more eager to volunteer the particulars of his day-to-day world.

Bedtimes provide another natural situation on which parents capitalize for intimate contact. Although a quick kiss and tuck-in is tempting for parents exhausted from a long workday, most working couples we interviewed said they try to spend several moments alone with each child before lights out. Matthew gets a choice of Bible stories before prayers. Other families have rituals, like special books of bedtime stories, or affirmation exercises like, "One thing I like about Daddy is ———" A favorite treat for Matthew is for one of us to linger after lights out and sit on the bed with him occasionally for a five-minute story about "something Mommy [or Daddy] did when she [or he] was a child."

Although weekday evenings are a virtual washout for

family time after dinner's cooked and dishes are put away, there still are a few activities that can usually salvage an evening for us. Matthew's favorite is to get out the slide projector for thirty minutes of photos, complete with popcorn and hot chocolate. Besides giving us a chance to dust off the slide trays, it also provides an occasion to reminisce about trips to Disneyland or what Matthew did when he was a baby.

A book called *Prime Time Parenting* by Dr. Kay Kuzma is one of the best we've seen, with suggestions for turning even the most prosaic moment—such as peeling potatoes or sitting in a dentist's waiting room—into a special memory for a child who has less than the average amount of time to spend with his parents.[8]

## Time for Each Other

As we looked for two-paycheck couples to interview, I called a minister friend for the names of some working couples who might be signed up for his next marriage-enrichment retreat. Both he and I were dismayed to see there were no such couples on his list. What we discovered may reflect a broader trend among two-paycheck couples in general: when the calendar is full, the marriage takes a back-row seat.

Working couples often find they need to put a note on their bathroom mirror that reads, "Husbands and wives need love, too." The combination of work and family takes a demanding toll, and couples must constantly be on the lookout for ways to replenish their marriage. As with children, quality time for spouses doesn't just happen; it takes strategy and planning.

Linda and Larry Calvert said they program in time together by having coffee outdoors on their deck every evening after work—a habit they cultivated early in their marriage and were determined to continue after daughter Lindsay was born. "It's our special time to find out where each person is," said Larry. The Calverts also bought a van so they can be alone together one weekend a month, away from the telephone, housework, and the routine of living.

The thirty minutes of freeway commuting before we arrive at Matthew's school every evening is the time Kay and I use to touch base. We rely on that time to get all the "shop talk" out of the way, so that we don't have to bore Matthew with a litany of grown-up conversation. By the time we have him in tow, we're ready to move on to subjects that include him.

One working husband and wife whose oldest child can reliably be left in charge for about forty-five minutes enjoy jogging together in the early mornings before their work days begin. This same family automatically signs up a baby sitter each week so they can go out to dinner or to the show on Saturday night. (They spend Saturday afternoon with the kids playing miniature golf or some other family-time activity.)

Harriett and Floyd Thatcher, who have written a book on the ingredients of long-term marriage, say there are certain key words that describe marriages that are alive, growing, and enduring. These words are authenticity, openness, caring, faith, and confidence. The Thatchers said these five qualities "bring to the marriage relationship a homeostatic quality in which two committed people can maintain an equilibrium based on a balanced and conscious attention to these characteristics."[9] If a working husband and wife want their marriage to thrive in the face of a draining schedule, they must protect some regular time to spend together, communicating on a deeper level than that of children's carpools and grocery lists.

## Friendships

It used to be so easy to make and keep friends when you were a child: you'd just go out in the front yard, start making mudpies, and soon a whole gang of neighborhood urchins would be wallowing in the mud alongside you. But in adulthood—especially when the adults are working couples—friendships often become a casualty of out-of-control schedules. Coworkers can fill part of that gap, as camaraderie develops by working together. But working relationships cannot take the place of personal friendships that have developed over the years and that now go begging because a working couple feels they should spend any spare moment with each other and with the children.

Counselor Lavonia Duck had this comment on friends she keeps up with by mail: "Part of my ministry is corresponding with people. As I would add new friends, my list of people to write would grow longer. Now, I'm no longer able to keep the pace, so I trimmed my mailing list considerably. I took the time that I might spend on that writing and now I invest it in a present friend."

Elaborate entertaining, which Lavonia and her husband Roger once relied on to keep friendships alive, also falls off when both spouses work. "You don't have the energy to go on a big housecleaning blitz and fix a fancy dinner to invite friends over, so friendships suffer," she said. As a way to keep and cultivate friendships, Lavonia suggested that two-paycheck couples think of alternatives when entertaining. "Use paper plates and everyone bring something; go out to lunch or arrange to meet your friends for lunch if you can't have them over on weekends or during the evenings."

To avoid insulting a friend over a forgotten birthday or other occasion, Linda King said she "shops sales and stocks up on baby and wedding gifts and Hallmark cards for every occasion. Then, when they announce at church that someone is sick or someone's shower is tomorrow, I don't have to get frantic." Kay prides herself on having not forgotten a birthday since she started buying a full year's supply of cards. In January of each year, she spends an entire lunch hour at a card store with calendar in hand, selecting cards for everyone on her birthday list. Once labeled and stuffed in a special monthly file, she makes periodic checks and pulls the card out when it's time.

One working spouse team who puts a high premium on friendships watches the paper for "two for the price of one" pizza coupons, and uses the occasion to invite another couple to go along. It's a low-cost way of keeping friendships vital without a lot of entertainment hassle on anyone's part.

## Making Sunday Go Better

Several years ago, I spent a Friday in the home of an Orthodox rabbi. I marveled as the rabbi, his wife, and their maid scurried about the house getting ready for the Sabbath, which begins at sundown on Fridays. By late Friday afternoon, the rabbi's house was spotless. The table in the dining room had been set with the best china and silver. In the kosher kitchen a variety of foods were warming in slow cookers. Shortly before sundown, everyone dressed in his or her best clothing. When the Sabbath began, everything in the rabbi's home was ready for a day of rest and worship and freedom from any domestic chores. Because of preparation and planning, the Sabbath went smoothly.

We feel that two-paycheck couples can benefit from planning for their times of worship, just as Orthodox Jews prepare their homes and selves for the coming of the Sabbath. In our interviews, we learned numerous methods two-paycheck couples use to simplify their Sundays (or other day of worship) and to make it as serene and pleasant as possible.

Linda and Eric King said they have discovered that the best way to include church in their busy schedule without becoming too frantic or rushed is to have a regular Sunday morning routine. Linda gave us this account: "Each person wakes on his own, except Cory, aged four. Eric usually wakes at seven-thirty and reads the Sunday paper till eight. I like to sleep till eight. That's late for us. We have a rule that there is no reading the newspaper past eight. Before we even wake Cory, we set out her Sunday clothes. [This differs from the Kings' weekday schedule, when Cory gets to choose her own clothes.] She dresses herself. On Sunday mornings, breakfast is optional. Usually, the kids fix themselves cereal—or, when they're acting weird, a grilled cheese sandwich in the microwave. Eric and I do without [breakfast] or have toast. Each person gets his own Bible, contribution, and lesson book. We still take a little bag with small books, puzzles, and goodies in it for Cory, to amuse her during church, before the little kids are dismissed for children's church."

Donna and Bob Oates said they've found that it helps make Sunday go better to "try and finish all chores before Sunday." That way, they are more relaxed and ready for church on Sunday mornings. On Sundays, they use the team spirit that they've adopted on weekdays. Bob fixes breakfast for the family while Donna dresses and makes up the beds. To avoid complications, Donna and Bob plan a light meal for lunch after church. Donna said they usually have salad and sandwiches, which makes for less hassle.

At the Oates' household, Sunday afternoon is set aside for rest. "There is nothing better than a Sunday afternoon nap," said Donna.

Royce Smith said she and husband Skip "do our best to relax on Sunday and make it in every sense the Lord's Day." She said they "lay out clothes for the children on Saturday night." On Sunday morning Royce puts a roast on. It will cook while the family is at church, so that when they come home, dinner is nearly ready and they can have a more leisurely afternoon.

Sandra and Curtis Lengefeld rely on fast-food restaurants to make their noon meal preparation on Sunday go smoothly. ("We have no big breakfast on Sunday mornings," said Sandra.) They also make sure everyone washes his or her hair on Saturday night, so there will be less confusion in the bathrooms on Sunday morning.

Maggie and Jim Barber said they've discovered two important rules for making Sunday go better: they get to bed early on Saturday nights, and they set the alarm on Sunday mornings. Sharon and John Lawson also said learning to "get up early" on Sunday mornings is the key to a successful church life for them. Attending their church's earliest service on Sunday is another favorite two-paycheck family trick for adding extra hours to Sundays. This practice usually frees the two-paycheck family by about eleven in the morning instead of the usual twelve-thirty.

Several couples we interviewed said they have learned over the years to plan ahead for their Sunday morning church responsibilities. Vicki Black said she reads her Sunday school literature at work during her lunch break. Her husband Mike said he takes along his church literature to study between sales calls. Ann Sullivan said she plans ahead for the lessons she teaches in her church's Sunday school. "I go through all the lessons for a quarter and make my plans all at once," she said. Ann said she also relies on letters to stay in contact with teachers in her Sunday school department. In that way, she said, she can skip Wednesday night teachers' meeting. "You can tell them (the other teachers) just as much in a letter as you can in person," she said.

Sandra Lengefeld saves all her Sunday school materials in her "church closet" at home to use from year to year; this keeps her from having to "reinvent the wheel" with each new group. Her husband Curtis said he tries to schedule Sunday school parties for his boys' class immediately after the worship service instead of on a weekend or weeknight. "My time-saving theory is, 'Just use Sunday; when you've got them there together, keep them.'"

Quiet time and personal meditation is a crucial spiritual need that often gets lost in the crush of the two-paycheck lifestyle. The period I spend jogging each morning is my special time to center down on spiritual needs. Kay often takes extended baths because she finds it's her only time of day to be totally alone for spiritual thoughts and prayer. A Methodist friend and two-paycheck family member in my office used to spend the first few minutes of his work day reading items that were important to his faith.

The schedules of two-paycheck families are hectic, but however they do it, the couples we interviewed said they found it possible to make time for spiritual enrichment. Each of us needs a spiritual life. Without it, we are not the person God wants us to be. All of us, not just two-paycheck families, need to remember the words of Jesus in Matthew 6:33: "But seek ye first the kingdom of God and his righteousness; and all these things shall be added unto you" (KJV).

# 9. Fathers: A Crucial Factor

Mary Frances Henry travels frequently in her job as a consultant and seminar leader. Nonworking mothers in her Presbyterian church who know of her travel schedule often pummel her with questions like, "How can you manage to get away from your three kids? How do they feel about your being gone?"

To this, Mary Frances has a stock reply: "They have a father, too, you know."

In one sentence, this working mother hit on a major cornerstone in the successful lifestyle of a two-paycheck family: both spouses must be active, involved members of the parenting team, with neither the father nor mother taking less than a quarterback's role.

In Chapter 8, we discussed how team participation in household tasks—the nitty-gritty of cleaning, laundering, and cooking—was crucial to two-paycheck couples who want to include church in their balancing act. If both husband and wife pitch in without regard to sex stereotypes, chores are done twice as fast, with more time to devote to activities, such as church, that are meaningful to the whole family.

As our interviews progressed, we confirmed another trend. A key to keeping a two-paycheck family in balance is the commitment of the fathers in these marriages to sharing responsibility for their children. And because fathers are "in there," taking up the slack—not only helping out with children while mothers run errands but actually spending ongoing quality time with the children to strengthen father-child relationships—these families find that staying active in church is easier for the whole family. Mothers are less likely to wake up on Sunday mornings wrestling guilt pangs and thinking, "Oh dear, Johnny hasn't had my attention this week. I'd better skip Sunday school today." If Johnny's father has been in the parenting game all week, too—capitalizing on those precious and fleeting moments when Johnny needed nurturing and doing all those tasks that previously were for mothers only—then both parents rest easier about the time they feel church might take away from their family. The father's role seems to be such a key to the two-paycheck family being able to manage a hectic schedule and to include church in it that we felt the issue should be singled out for a separate chapter here.

## An Unexpected Bonanza

Critics, especially those found in churches, often say their main objection to the two-paycheck lifestyle is "what it will do to the home and the family." Somehow, these skeptics have become frozen in a negative focus. They fear that the family will be wrecked when the mother gives less than full-time attention to housework and children. In so doing, these critics often ignore the flip side of the coin—the fact that the working-mother boom may be just what the doctor ordered to correct a well-documented family problem—the emotionally-detached husband and father.

This type of absentee father is a well-known product of our modern era. He grew out of the same factors that spawned the "traditional" one-paycheck family with Dad at work and Mom at home. In earlier times, fathers usually worked close to home and were more involved with their families on a daily basis. Fathers taught their children various trades, such as carpentry, farming or watchmaking. The family often lived on a farm or in quarters near or even above the father's shop. Fathers usually came home for lunch and often were only a few hundred yards away for regular interaction.

But with the arrival of the Industrial Revolution, which literally overhauled society, fathers began taking jobs that usually removed them physically and emotionally from their families. The advent of the automobile and new superhighways capped these changes and cemented them in concrete. Cities boomed, and "bedroom communities," where moms and kids lived in a separate world all day while Dad commuted to a faraway downtown office building or industrial plant, sprang up overnight and, by the 1950s, had become an American way of life. Men became caught up in the "get ahead" syndrome, working extra hours to show their dedication to their companies and to their jobs. Many spent weekends at the office in order to climb the ladder of success. In an era of burgeoning material possessions, many fathers separated themselves from active, daily family time and became partial strangers to their children while they slaved to provide "the better things" that they thought would add to their family's quality of life.

Besides being provider and breadwinner, the only other role of the father in this era was that of strict disciplinarian. Father was frequently shrouded in the "just wait until your father gets home" image; he was known as the person who regularly took off his belt and "tanned" young "hides" for some wrong committed while he was away at work. In addition, "many fathers were taught to present, especially to their sons, a stiff-lipped model of what it is to 'be a man,' which meant, in traditional role terms, sticking to business, resisting the influence of feelings, and knowing little of the emotional life of others, or even of their own deeper emotions."[1]

Furthermore, under this type of regimen, fathers were seldom alone with their children, except maybe in rare structured situations such as a camping trip or a "father-child" banquet at church or school. Then, the two often sat stone-faced, struggling for something to talk about, because being together was so rare. Fathers sometimes responded with resentment and even horror to such occasions because they seemed so awkward. For in this era, the mother had taken over as the primary parent—the one who soothed all the hurts, dealt with all the school matters, and refereed all the neighborhood squabbles. Dad was not to be bothered with such matters when he came home and escaped into the blare of his TV set or hid behind a newspaper. On weekends, if he wasn't back at the office, he was likely to conveniently remove himself to the golf course.

Sociologists and psychologists soon realized the problems that these emotionally absent fathers were creating. A 1974 study by Urie Bronfenbrenner showed that the typical middle-class father of a one-year-old child spent an average of 37.7 seconds per day interacting with his infant.[2] About this same time, in 1974, Henry Biller and Dennis Meredith wrote the book, *Father Power*, to document the crucial roles fathers play in the lives of children of both sexes. In their masterful and monumental report, the authors showed that when the quality of fathering increased, so did the overall mental health of boys and girls, men and women. They also claimed that a child may be harmed more by having an emotionally absent father than he or she would be by having no father at all in the home.[3]

## A New Awakening

The Bronfenbrenner and Biller-Meredith studies seemed to coincide with a renewed awareness of the importance of fathers. Suddenly, dads began appearing in hospital delivery rooms, as Lamaze and other childbirth techniques featuring husbands as coaches and active supporters in the birthing process became popular. Baby-care books began hinting that someone besides Mom might be able to change

diapers, and even television advertisements began showing
dads choosing clothes for their young daughters and sons.
Courts began awarding custody of children to fathers in
increasing numbers, as dads started proving that they too
could be the nurturing primary parent. By the end of the
1970s, publishing houses were churning out books by the
dozens on fathering. Sermons, newspaper articles, and lec-
tures on the subject became almost commonplace. The era
of the father was in full bloom by the early 1980s. The
Reverend Jesse Jackson, a well-known black Baptist minister and civil rights leader, summarized this new trend in
this statement to a group of fathers, "Your children need
your presence more than your presents."⁴ The words of
another relevant slogan that became popular during the late
1970s also said it well: "The best thing to spend on children
is your time."

## Fathers in the Bible

The revived emphasis on the father's role today meshes
well with what the Bible seems to envision for men who
are parents. Fathering is presented in the Bible as more
than a simple act of fertilization or insemination. Fathers
in the Bible were significant figures in the lives of their
children. In fact, whole books could be written just about
fathers in the Bible. Adam, Abraham, Isaac, Jacob, Moses,
David and Joseph all were biblical fathers of significance.

In the Lord's Prayer, Jesus taught his followers to refer
to God as "Our Father which art in Heaven" (Luke 11:2,
KJV). Obviously Jesus, who frequently referred to God as
his father, knew the power and importance of fatherhood.
In fact, one of the great parables Jesus told was about a
man who was restored to a right relationship with his father.
That man was the Prodigal Son, and his story is found in
Luke 15:11–32. In this well-known and oft-quoted parable,
a father had two sons. One asked for his inheritance early
and left, only to squander the money in a far country. The

other stayed home with his father. Eventually the son who left returned asking to be hired as a servant. The father accepted the errant son back with great joy and forgiveness. But the elder brother objected to the father's seemingly inexhaustible love for his younger brother.

Thousands of sermons have been preached on the various aspects of this parable. But surely one of the most important points of the story is the picture it gives of God as loving, compassionate, and forgiving. These are characteristics a human father should have also. "The parent who fails to act like the father in the story of the Prodigal Son does himself and his children a disservice," says Howard Hovde, a Baptist minister and family counselor. "The father in this story was accepting. His son was reconciled to him. Never again could the relationship be the same between the two. The Prodigal had the choice of whether to come home and to be reconciled with his father. The father had the choice whether to make a reconciliation. Had they chosen otherwise, life for both would have somehow seemed devoid of joy and love." [5]

## An Important Expanding Role

The renewed emphasis on fathering dovetails appropriately with the two-paycheck lifestyle, which offers fathers many more opportunities to become as intimate with their children as mothers have always been. Since teamwork is the key to success in a two-paycheck family, in this type of marriage it is often the father who picks up the child from school, gives the bedtime bath, attends parent-teacher conferences, buys the new tennis shoes, and chauffeurs young musicians to piano lessons. Instead of merely helping out once in a while, fathers in two-paycheck families find themselves equally responsible for child-rearing chores. As a result, just from having more frequent exposure to their children, fathers now have a chance to be active participants in the lives of their offspring—to really crawl around inside their minds, to know their fears, their inhibitions, their strengths. What's more, in the two-paycheck family, fathers can learn things about their children firsthand, and not have to rely on Mom's daily observations. For example, if Johnny is having trouble getting along with Freddie at school, the father in a two-paycheck family is often there on the scene, observing the interaction and forming his own opinions of what the trouble may be. This way, he doesn't have to rely on the teacher's report or his wife's interpretation of the squabble.

A further advantage of the two-paycheck marriage is that such an arrangement gives a child the opportunity to see his mother and his father as whole persons, not just as fragmented stereotypes. A child whose mother works will grow up viewing women as not only nurturing, comforting, and domestic—qualities that have traditionally been ascribed to females—but also as assertive, decisive, and businesslike—qualities previously reserved for males. Conversely, the father takes on many facets in his children's eyes. A child in a two-paycheck family not only sees his father as independent and ambitious in his work, but also as tender and caring at home.[6] When Johnny sees Daddy making out the grocery list and Mommy bringing home a paycheck, he will be less likely to grow up with a narrow view of what men and women should be. He will learn to be sensitive to individual differences in people, to base his view of them not on a standard role but on the human, God-given qualities that make each person a unique creation.

I was fascinated when a friend of Matthew's who does not live in a two-paycheck family talked to me about why I had done the grocery shopping and was putting my purchases away in the cabinet. This child kept saying, "My daddy doesn't do the grocery shopping. Why did you? Is Matthew's mommy sick? Why isn't she doing this?" I was glad that this child had the opportunity to see that men, too, can perform these tasks, because otherwise she might grow up with the idea that grocery stores have a "No men allowed" sign on them.

Boys and girls who see their parents modeling a successful two-paycheck lifestyle will likely grow up more receptive to living in their own two-paycheck families as adults. We feel this is especially important, since the two-paycheck lifestyle is destined to become almost a necessity in the next generation. In our interviews, a number of husbands said they adjusted better to their present lifestyle because their own mothers had worked outside the home when they were young. My mother was employed when I was a child, and I too believe it has helped me take the idea of a working wife in stride. Kay and I have noted that men who were reared in two-paycheck homes tend to be less constrained by role stereotypes in their present homes and marriages. Mark Henry, one of those we interviewed who was reared in a two-paycheck home, supported this observation. As a youngster, he said, he learned to do various housekeeping chores: "I didn't know it was woman's work. I came into this marriage with less role-stereotyping than most men have."

## Some Firsthand Testimonies

Now, let's look at this new view of fathering through the eyes of some of the people we interviewed:

Larry Calvert took to fatherhood with the enthusiasm of a child at Christmas when he and his wife Linda became late-in-life parents of daughter Lindsay. At thirty-nine, Larry viewed fathering as an unexpected but welcome blessing and joy, and he spoke with unabashed zeal about the chances it afforded him. Moreover, instead of resenting the fact that his wife was not a stay-at-home mother, Larry seemed tickled that Linda's job as a college professor caused her to work some late evenings and to make out-of-town trips. To him, these times gave him but one more occasion to spend time alone with his darling little daughter.

"Larry refuses to be locked out of the places that are traditionally mine," said Linda. "When fathers talk about how they never change diapers, Larry gets irate because he says these folks are just cheating themselves. He demands the right to be a father and to have some of the goodies that the mother has."

If Bob Lobaugh had his "druthers," and family finances permitted, his wife Debbie would work only part-time, if at all. But that regret doesn't keep Bob from being thoroughly devoted to spending large chunks of time and doing his full share with their seven-year-old son Jermaine. "You have to work extra hard to make it up to a kid when his mother and father both work," he said. Bob felt he would be much more lax about hurrying through errands so time will be left for Jermaine if he knew that Debbie had been home with the youngster all day. And he admitted that being a member of a two-paycheck family has given him the opportunity to have a closer relationship with his son than he would have had if theirs followed the one-paycheck model.

Cecilia Valdes and Mike Rutledge, the engaged couple we interviewed, were so consumed with the idea of shared parenting that they already were mapping out plans for parenthood, even though they said children were at least eight years down the road for them.

"Because we both are planning active careers in medicine, we know our time with our children may be limited," said Cecilia. So they spent part of their engagement months interviewing other working couples, asking how they found time for family.

Mike said he would consider taking a guaranteed eight-to-five job, such as some sort of public-health position, after he and Cecilia have children, to make sure that they have a quality home life that does not get lost in the hubbub of having two parents constantly on call. "I want to be a doctor, but I want to be a good father, too," Mike said. "I'm not interested in getting rich or building up a large and well-known practice." He said he and Cecilia also have considered alternating work years when they have a family and accepting a lower standard of living in order to be more involved parents.

Judy and Jim Dougherty were so committed to the idea that children need quality time from both parents that they were considering cutting back both of their law practices into part-time jobs. "I'm not a workaholic, and I don't have any desire to be wealthy, but I feel the need to be with my family more," said Jim.

When Kay returned to work when Matthew was an infant, we found it helpful to spell out in a written contract some specific terms for our parenting. To make sure that Matthew got maximum available time from both his parents, we wrote down an entire day's schedule, detailing who would be with him at any given moment. To shorten the time we spent apart from him, we worked staggered schedules at the office. Since I left for work early, I could get free to pick him up earlier in the afternoon. Kay kept later hours, so she could drop him off at his nursery later in the morning. We also worked staggered days. Kay had Mondays off but worked Saturday nights, while I worked Monday through Friday. That way Matthew only had to be in day care for four days out of the week, and could have his parents' attention for three full days, instead of the normal two-day weekend.

We also had a detailed list for chores. For example, I would clean up the dinner dishes so that Kay could have a few minutes to romp on the floor with Matthew before his early bedtime. On Saturday mornings, we made sure that both of us ran errands at different times so that one of us was always giving him our virtual undivided attention. All this delicate planning had some real plusses for me— because I became a routine caregiver for our young son. I got to watch him emerge through all those early developmental stages—crawling, walking, finger feeding, drinking from a cup—that normally only a mother would witness.

I got to feel like I was an expert on early child development, too, and didn't just have to rely on my wife's impressions when I got home from work.

As Matthew grew older, of course, we relaxed this rigid schedule when we felt he no longer needed such intense parental contact, although we've basically continued to alternate time with him while one of us is writing or running errands. But we both doubt that we would have made it through those difficult first months after Kay returned to work when Matthew was one had we not known that our son was getting the most of what both his parents could offer—not just Mother, but Daddy too—in the time allotted. It was a key survival technique during a very crucial period for us.

Furthermore, we believe our system will build a communications bond that will pay off dividends in the long run. As Mary Jo and Wade Rowatt write, "A father who plays with his three-month-old or three-year-old child will have a thirteen-year-old who still likes to play with him." [7]

## Change Does Not Come Easy

Just as acceptance often comes at a snail's pace for the mother who returns to the job market, men who proclaim themselves as being intensely involved in fathering often face a few raised eyebrows. I experienced this the first time I told the men in my carpool that I would not be riding to work with them one morning because I had to take my son to the doctor. The next day I was in for some good-natured but very pointed ribbing. All these men, who basically fit the workaholic, emotionally absent father role, chided me about, "Where was your son's mother yesterday? Why couldn't *she* make the doctor's visit?"

I received a similar response the first time I phoned my city editor to say I needed to stay home from work to be with a sick child. The editor, who also was Kay's boss at the time, responded, "Gee, if Matthew is sick, I'll be glad to give Kay some time off to spend with him." After I thanked him but explained that I was the one whose interview schedule was most flexible that day, he agreed and after that never questioned us when we divided Matthew's sick days fifty-fifty. We felt that phone conversation with the city editor had engaged us in a bit of consciousness-raising about the new role of the father in a two-paycheck family.

Kay recently wrote a story about an unusual suburban neighborhood in which at least half the men on the block stayed home during the day while their wives held outside jobs. Some of the men were self-employed and ran their businesses in their own homes, while others had outside work with flexible hours, such as sales or airline piloting. But almost all of them took on the role as primary parent—in some cases caring for their children during the entire day while their wives worked away from home.

When Kay went to interview these men, however, only two out of seven were willing to be quoted on the record, with their actual names and photos in the newspaper. As one of the willing few explained, "These guys still have a particular way in which they want to be perceived by the public. They're still not comfortable with people knowing they're managing the home front."

One of the main criticisms of this new breed of father is that it produces men who are trying to be mothers. "For every liberated male who views without blanching the new nondifferentiation of labor, there are many more men and women who insist that there are vital, inherent differences between the two parental roles, and that to attempt to erase or ignore these differences is to risk a severe loss to human experience," write Hilary Ryglewicz and Pat Koch Thaler.[8] However, none of the men we encountered seemed intent on usurping the mother's role or cutting her out of something rightfully hers. The best fathering in the world won't make up for the lack of a mother—and vice versa. We believe that children, in order to flourish, need both parents devoting themselves to child-rearing at their fullest capacity.

As was true with the subject of working mothers, there never will be a time when all people embrace the concept of cooperative parenting, especially when the father exercises a nontraditional role. And if fathers wait until the full tide of public opinion turns in their favor, they may miss out on many precious and rewarding opportunities to be fully involved with their kids.

## So What Is a Father to Do?

What guidelines, then, can we offer the father in the two-paycheck family situation who wants to be more than an emotionally absent breadwinner or an occasional baby-sitter to his kids?

(1) *Expand your creative fathering skills.* If you've been in the figurehead father role for a while, and the whole idea of getting involved makes you feel panicky, there are many helpful publications now available to give dads some new tools for a better relationship. One of the best we've seen is *Dads Only,* a monthly newsletter for Christian fathers published by Paul Lewis and Ray Bruce, two dads in San Diego, California.[9] Not only does it offer practical tips for fun ways for dads and kids to spend time; it also suggests ways to get conversations going, hobbies that can be shared, and ways to capitalize on valuable times together like bed-time, meals, and errands. If you're looking for more creative ways to discipline other than the old swat-on-the-bottom technique, consider taking a parenting course with your wife, so you can be consistent in your methods of discipline and not work at cross-purposes to one another.

(2) *Learn to speak up to other men (especially those at church) about what you are doing with your children.* Fathers who are new to the game of involved fathering like to feel there's safety in numbers. If they know that other fathers chase around on their coffee breaks trying to locate Godzilla lunch boxes

for their six-year-old, they're more likely to volunteer for these necessary errands, too, to make their two-paycheck lifestyle go smoothly. So if you're among the involved, don't keep it quiet. I'll never forget how comforting it was to see two other fathers seated in the doctor's office the first time I took Matthew in to be treated for an ear infection. In chatting with these men, I learned that neither was a single parent who had no other person around to bring his children in; both were members of two-paycheck families. In one case, the father was the logical parent to do doctor's-office duty because his own office was only a few blocks away. The other man was a salesman who happened to have the afternoon free. As I saw how relaxed these two men were in their fathering roles, my tension eased, too.

(3) *Instead of complaining, reframe the situation and consider the important role you play* in trailblazing and making things better for this new generation of fathers. As more and more men pile into doctors' waiting rooms, physicians will learn to leave off the phrase, "Now tell the child's mother . . ." before giving instructions. As more men attend parent-teacher conferences and see that Dad is genuinely concerned about Johnny's writing problems or whatever, teachers will learn to begin taking the male parent as seriously as they do the female parent. An example of this occurred when Matthew was one, shortly after Kay returned to work. On occasion I would arrive at his day-care center to find fewer teachers on duty than the state child welfare laws mandated. Kay and I both protested to the local directors but got no response. So one day I picked up the phone and called the president of the day-care-center chain in California, and had a serious chat with him about state laws and student-teacher ratios in our local center. I had a copy of the state's day care licensing statutes in my hand, and there was little arguing he could do. He seemed astounded that a father would be so knowledgeable and would call him long distance. That evening the problems at the center were

corrected. I was pleased that I as a father could be effective in our arrangements for our son's care.

(4) *Consider how much you're learning.* I'm grateful to be just as informed as my wife is on what is needed for Matthew's care. When Matthew wakes with a cough in the middle of the night, I'm grateful I know immediately which antihistamine and how many aspirin to give him, without being in the dependent position of begging this information from his mother. I'm glad that I can intelligently discuss the teaching methods used at Matthew's school, and that I'm just as skilled as my wife is in knowing which discipline methods work best. I feel that being an involved father in every sense of the word makes me a more well-rounded, self-assured human being.

(5) *Help your church to help fathers who may need a little prodding to become more effective.* We believe cooperative parenting is the best arrangement, even in one-paycheck families. Fathers in traditional families in which the wives don't work outside the home can benefit from a little stimulation as well as can fathers in two-paycheck marriages.

Encourage your church leaders to offer study courses on fathering. As Mary Jo and Wade Rowatt put it, "Churches can help liberate men to be caring, giving, feeling persons. Jesus led His disciples to be examples of men free from the narrow restrictions that typed men as uncaring, selfish, nonfeeling individuals who must be aggressive, successful and always self-confident."[10] Caring, giving, feeling men make the best fathers; sometimes all they need is a little boost to bring these traits out of the closet and to know these qualities are acceptable for persons of either sex. Churches can play a key role in easing them into this new and exciting kind of fatherhood.

# 10. Hope for the Future

Kay had just finished another talk to a women's mission group on the subject of the church and the two-paycheck family. She shared with the women that she considered her work to be a calling, in the same sense that ministers are called. She told about some of the opportunities her job presents for Christian witness. She talked about some of the struggles we've had as a nontraditional family trying to keep the church a part of our lives.

Afterwards, a woman who had been quiet during the question-and-answer session thanked Kay for the speech. "It's been a real eye-opener to me," the woman said. "I just didn't realize that Christian women worked."

The comment startled Kay initially. Later, thinking about it, she realized it illustrated how misunderstood the two-paycheck family is in the church, and how much ground the two-paycheck family still has to cover in dealing with fellow church members.

Even though both husband and wife are now breadwinners in millions of U.S. families, representing nearly every denomination, some people, like the woman at Kay's meeting, may still have trouble accepting the two-paycheck lifestyle as a valid one for church people. Many people, including those in churches, have blind spots about any lifestyle that differs from the norm, and they still view the two-paycheck situation as questionable. In some circles, working couples face a stern challenge to show by their example that it is indeed possible for marriage partners to be in the labor market, maintain a healthy marriage relationship, and still have close ties with a church.

## Encouraged By Our Interviews

Even though churches may be a real pioneer area for working couples, we were encouraged by our interviews. The people we talked to proved to us that progress is being made, even in the most staid of congregations. Although sometimes the gains they reported were small, our couples gave us a general feeling of hope. They spoke of doors being opened in churches that we would have never dreamed possible just five years ago. They told us of stereotypes falling, attitudes changing and an embryonic tolerance starting to take hold. They showed that their perseverence in keeping involved at church was beginning to pay off slight, though crucial, dividends, as fellow church members became less defensive toward them.

In addition, the people we interviewed showed us that the issue of two-paycheck families is much more complex than simple liberal-versus-conservative philosophy. Many of the couples we interviewed would be classified as politically and theologically conservative, as would the congregations they attend. Yet they and their churches were adapting to a way of living that is often labeled as liberal.

## Church Leaders Make a Difference

Some people we talked with credited their pastors and other church leaders with supportive acts that gave them good feelings about what they were trying to do.

Accountant Barbara Myers said she gets "good vibes" from the pastor of her Presbyterian congregation when he introduces her to others as "the financial person in our church." She said she felt this was an important way of signifying that he sanctioned her using her talents in finance to the fullest.

Similarly, psychiatric nurse Janet Zaozirny felt that appointing her to the call committee for a new counseling pastor in her Lutheran church was a vote of confidence by the church leadership. In her mind, utilizing her special training by putting her on the important committee was a powerful "you're OK" statement.

Teacher Sandra Lengefeld said her Baptist church's educational director "has singled me out as an example when he's talking to others [about working women]. He tells them that I'm definitely someone who works outside the home but can still fit church into my schedule." She felt such affirmation would make it easier for others in her church to accept the two-paycheck family concept.

Our pastor, Ken Chafin, is one of the most sensitive and conscientious ministers we've ever known in dealing with the two-paycheck lifestyle, and he has been enormously supportive in our particular situation. I cover religion for the largest newspaper in Texas and deal with Ken routinely on religion news, but he calls Kay with secular story ideas for the Lifestyle section of the newspaper almost as frequently as he calls me on religious matters. When he does so, Kay said he shows remarkable news judgment; almost every idea he suggests to her eventually turns into a legitimate story.

Furthermore, Ken routinely comments from the pulpit about byline articles we've each had in the newspaper, and often ties them into his sermon topics in ways which amaze us. Despite his busy schedule, we've found Ken to be a voracious newspaper reader. When he remarks to us about stories we've written, it's obvious to us that he's done more than just a cursory scanning of the material and has thought out our work carefully.

Kay particularly appreciates such attention because she believes it adds to the overall acceptance we've found at our church for our two-paycheck lifestyle. By holding up professional women as role models, and by making sermon references to women who perform jobs besides homemaking, a pastor creates a positive atmosphere in which the two-paycheck lifestyle can thrive without censure. Furthermore, when such an attitude starts with the minister, it is more likely to be picked up and reflected by other members of the church staff. Women in the congregation who may be trying to decide whether they should take outside employment will feel much more comfortable if they see such work validated by an admired pastor who's a significant figure in their lives. They will be much less likely to be shackled by guilt when they return to the market place if ministers' sermons do not set up the "husband at work, wife at home" model as the only valid lifestyle.

It's amazing how just a few scattered references to women as doctors instead of housewives, or to dads instead of moms attending a parent-teacher conference, can go a long way toward raising people's consciousness and exposing them to other options. We were thrilled that one of our pastor's principal examples in his Labor Day sermon recently was a very energetic and aggressive woman in a traveling sales job—a relatively new field for females to enter. We feel that such illustrations are important, since Labor Day sermons are usually addressed to men who work. Such an attitude as displayed in this pastor's sermon can go a long way toward fostering equality in church situations.

Not all the people we talked to, however, expect or even want overt affirmation of their two-paycheck lifestyle from their church leaders. Some said they prefer ministers who keep out of the whole issue. They don't want their ministers to affirm or condemn their lifestyle, but just to keep silent on the issue. "It's not what our minister says; it's what he doesn't say," said Martha Haun, a college professor and member of a Church of Christ. "He simply has a live-and-let-live attitude; he leaves us alone about our lifestyle and makes no judgment, and that's what counts."

And there are people like schoolteacher Ann Sullivan who don't feel the need for nods of approval from their church leaders. Ann said she feels secure enough in her lifestyle that she doesn't look for special attention from her Baptist pastor or the other ministers on her church's large staff.

But whether their church leaders gave tacit or overt support to the two-paycheck lifestyle, most of the interviewees wanted their ministers to at least regard them on their own merits as individuals and to not brand them with some unfair "working woman" label that would single them out from the rest of the congregation.

## Group Support Is Sometimes Important

Many couples we interviewed see hope for the future of the two-paycheck couple and the church in the way their church friends and church organizations have responded to accommodate their schedules.

For example, Vicki Black said that, instead of leaning on her to prepare food as they once did when she was a full-time homemaker, her fellow church members ask her only "to chip in money to help buy a ham" when there's a death in their Church of Christ congregation. "At showers, if I happen to be a hostess, friends will say, 'Since you work, why don't you be the one to bring napkins and peanuts this time?' "

Royce Smith was flattered when her Baptist Sunday school class scheduled a daytime luncheon "about a mile from where I work so that I could go." And on a recent prayer retreat, "they arranged to take two vans—one at 4:00 P.M. to take those who don't have outside jobs and another at 6:00 P.M. to pick up working people so we could go later."

Donna Oates felt the cause of working women got a shot in the arm and a vote of confidence at her Baptist church when the missions group began an annual luncheon to honor Christian educators like herself. Furthermore, because of the increasing numbers of employed women in the church, Sunday school meetings which once were all daytime luncheons are now being held at night every other month. And instead of disbanding in May, these meetings are now held throughout the summer—the only time working women who are teachers can attend regularly.

Another helpful rescheduling occurred at Lou and James Barron's Episcopal church, which moved Wednesday night teachers' meetings to Sunday mornings before Bible study to help out working folks who couldn't make the night sessions.

Sandra Lengefeld said the most helpful support of her lifestyle from the church occurred when her Baptist church friends offered to babysit for her youngest son when he was sick. "Church friends often have kept him when I'm in-between sitters," she said. "I couldn't work if I didn't have them to rely on." We found the Lengefelds' experience a welcome contrast to our own earlier church experiences, in which we experienced only hostility and raised eyebrows from our "church friends" about day-care arrangements.

We know of one Baptist church in our community that plans a special day camp in the summer as a ministry to children of working parents. The church provides a safe, healthy environment during long, hot Gulf Coast summer days when working couples must make special arrangements to care for their school-aged children.

Methodist Nora Bishop said she felt particularly affirmed when her Sunday school class members tossed her a party when she graduated from nursing school. And Debbie Lobaugh said she appreciates the effort her Baptist Sunday school class makes to notify her about daytime parties, even if party plans are not altered to account for her work schedule. "They say, 'We know you work, but if there's any way you can get off, we'd like you to come.' At least I'm not being ignored. At least they're trying to reach out to me."

The working wives we interviewed were grateful for all these efforts to include them and to make it easier for them to be involved in church activities. But Royce Smith spoke for many when she added that she doesn't always expect— or want—to be catered to because she is a working mother. "They were signing up people to bring refreshments for my daughters' mission group and they asked me to bring punch. I said, 'Why are you asking me to bring punch, since I've always brought cookies?' They said, 'Because you work.' It hurt my feelings. I didn't want to be left out. I told them to continue to call on me for cookies."

## What's Being Overlooked

Most of the couples we talked with felt there is a growing acceptance of the two-paycheck lifestyle in the church today. Several couples, however, spoke wistfully of things they feel would make them more comfortable as a two-paycheck family in a church setting.

The way new church members are introduced in a congregation has special significance to Kay and to several of the other working women we interviewed, because they feel the accepted method represents an attitude which needs changing. "It's always 'This is Mr. and Mrs. John Jones. He's the vice president down at the bank and they have two children.' Well, who is Mrs. Jones? Does she have a first name? And what if she's a Ph.D. at the college in town? Doesn't she deserve to have that fact known about her, too?" says Kay. Though it's a trival matter to some folks, Kay feels that churches could show their support of employed couples and of women in general just by changing this one perfunctory practice.

Adopting a "team teaching" approach for Sunday school also would be helpful for two-paycheck families who need some weekend flexibility, said lawyer Judy Doughtery. "This way a person could alternate responsibility with someone. If churches made being active come across in a way that wouldn't seem like such a huge commitment, then more people would be eager to do church work."

In their book on two-paycheck families, Mary Jo and Wade Rowatt confirm this point. Recognizing that the return of women to the job market may cut into the number of available church volunteer help, they make this suggestion: "If the faithful could be used to enlist more helpers for less time, then the churches would be more stable and couples could also be under less overload."[1]

Two-paycheck couples should be regular speakers at church seminars for newlyweds, Ann Sullivan suggested. She said that when people get married, they need to know right off what peculiar stresses two jobs bring to a lifestyle. Ann would also like her church to offer marriage enrichment retreats strictly for the two-paycheck teams in the congregation. "These couples have pressures traditional families can't identify with," she said. As churches broaden the focus on family life, she feels, the hurts and needs of working couples cannot be overlooked in the family life education process.

Journalists Gay McFarland and John Scarborough, the working husband and wife who were looking for church again after a long period of being non-attenders, said they would be more likely to join a church with services that start at noon or 1:00 P.M., since John works as an amusements critic and often doesn't get home from his Saturday night reviews until the wee hours of the morning. A midday or early afternoon service also would help working couples whose only night to go on "dates" is Saturday. It would keep them from having to make the either/or choice of "Do we take in a movie tonight or stay home so we can make it to church tomorrow?"

Working parents with small children also could benefit from an afternoon Sunday service, said jeweler Meg Elliott. "That's the time our son takes his nap. He could be in the church nursery sleeping while we were at worship. Then we wouldn't miss out on family time together when he's awake on Sundays."

Gay and John also said they would appreciate a parents' night out that churches could offer as an adjunct to "mother's day out" for full-time homemakers. They feel a church shouldn't limit its short-term babysitting services just to women who need time away from their children during the day. "The thing that working parents need most is some time together away from both work and kids," said Gay.

Mary Jo and Wade Rowatt suggest in *The Two-Career Marriage* that churches condense some activities to have a wide variety of programs all on the same night (a somewhat expanded program of our church's Friday Night Live) so that couples aren't expected to spend every night of the week running to and from meetings.[2] They envisioned an evening beginning with a fellowship meal and then offering Bible study, music, mission emphasis, prayer groups, or recreational activities.

The Church of Jesus Christ of Latter-day Saints recently tried a version of this when it reorganized its Sunday program to reduce the number of times a family must travel to and from church. By placing all Sunday activities into one three-hour block of time, the Mormons hope to reduce gasoline expenses, save the cost of heating and air conditioning their buildings several times on Sunday, and to give families more time together on the Lord's Day. Though Mormons are not strong advocates of the two-paycheck lifestyle, we feel their scheduling concept for Sundays is something that could be adapted to help working couples.

The Rowatts also recommend in their book that churches could help working couples by planning growth groups in which four or six two-paycheck couples would meet together regularly for sharing—especially during the first year or so that they are adjusting to the lifestyle.[3] Couples could exchange ideas on how to make it all work—from child care to domestic tasks and bolstering each other when they're feeling down. We feel this idea is helpful because, although we do not know of a specific study to back us up, we believe the success or failure of the two-paycheck lifestyle is determined in the first year after the arrangement is begun. The working couple must either adapt to the new schedule and develop routines that will help their lifestyle succeed, or they will fail. By setting up programs such as the Rowatts recommend, the church can become a supportive element and a factor in ensuring the success of the two-paycheck lifestyle.

Patsy Blackwood, a Houston counselor and member of the Christian Church (Disciples of Christ) who also is a member of a two-paycheck family, said in a newspaper interview that churches wanting to minister to working couples must learn to emphasize the *quality* of time one spends at church, not the *amount* of time. She said many churchgoers want intimacy and deep personal relationships. "Large amounts of time spent together does not equal intimacy. The quality of time together is what's important."

In the same interview, Blackwood and Jim Killen, pastor of a Methodist church in Houston, said churches may need to add additional paid staff persons to take care of duties—such as cooking, maintenance and some secretarial work—which in the past were done by volunteers. "If the two-career family tithes their extra money, there should be no problem in making changes in this area," said Killen.[4]

## What Can You Do To Help?

What can you as an individual church member or couple do to help the cause of two-paycheck families in your church? Look at your own congregation as a mission field and consider yourself a missionary to spread the important news about a lifestyle that may seem foreign to many churchgoers, just as it was to the woman we mentioned at the opening of this chapter. Ask your church friends for help, but don't expect them to automatically take up the cause with you, especially if they are members of one-paycheck households. Here are a few suggestions for ways to take action:

(1) *Get a dialogue going with your minister.* Talk to him individually, or round up several couples who share your concerns and make an appointment. If some of the suggestions in this chapter strike a receptive chord with you, present them to him, and tell him why you think they are worth a try. People in the clergy sincerely want their programs to meet the congregation's needs. Ministers know that a responsive church yields happier parishioners, and happy parishioners yield growth and harmony in the church. If you feel your church staff has a blind spot when it comes to two-paycheck families, talk about it with the pastor. See if together you can hammer out some ideas that will meet everyone's needs and will make two-paycheck families feel more a part of the church's programs.

(2) *If your church has a library, suggest that your librarian obtain books about the two-paycheck lifestyle the next time he or she wants to expand the family life section.* Those books we have mentioned as resources in these chapters would be excellent starters. Family life issues are extremely hot topics nowadays, so make sure your library doesn't overlook working couples when stocking its shelves.

(3) *Appoint yourself as a two-paycheck family watchdog in your church.* If you notice in your congregation's newsletter that an event is consistently held at a time not convenient to working couples, call it to someone's attention. If your church has nursery space that is standing idle during the week, find out why it's never been turned into a day-care center for children of working parents or into a space for afterschool supervision. If your church regularly sponsors a family life weekend but does not include a workshop on the two-paycheck lifestyle, offer to find a speaker. If you hear attitudes espoused in sermons that seem to restrict male and female roles, discuss them with your minister. You may not change his mind, but you can alert him to the fact that there are other ways of viewing the issue.

(4) *Remember that the most crucial action you can take in your church occurs on a one-to-one basis.* As we wrote in the opening illustration of this book, interpersonal relationships had the most hurtful impact on us as we struggled to be a working couple who are active in a church. Relationships can also be the factor that keeps a working couple involved in church! Seek out families in your church's membership who are in transition to the two-paycheck lifestyle. Encourage them. Tell them it can work. Offer to babysit on a weekend in the near future so they can go out alone and regroup. I saw a plaque recently which said, "Compassion is the pain you feel when someone else hurts." Look back on your own experiences and seek out others who may hurt as you did once. Make sure they know they can count on you as a supporter. In the long run, your help may make a difference between the success and failure of their decision.

## Don't Give Up on the Church!

As we have detailed in these chapters, there was a time when we wondered whether there was room in the church for the two-paycheck family. Happily, because of our interviews and our own experiences, we can now say unequivocally that there is! The two-paycheck family can still have a rewarding church relationship, even though their lifestyle may not be the norm in their congregation. We rejoice in this because our faith in something we hold dear—the church—has been restored. And because of our experiences, we adjure other Christian working couples: Don't give up on your lifestyle or on the church. As Elton Trueblood writes, "Even though it is normally much adulterated, the church is now, as always, the saving salt. The intelligent plan, then, is never to abandon the church, but instead to find some way of restoring the salt."[5]

A *Christianity Today* editorial carries this thought a step further: "This helpless, confused, sin-ridden, even, at times repulsive institution, Jesus Christ not only established; he also promised to stand behind it, and to protect it against all its foes to the very end of time. Of course the church is worth serving and saving not because of what it is, but because of who Jesus Christ is and because of the relationship that church bears to him."[6]

For people who love Jesus Christ, being active and committed church members is the only answer; there is little happiness to be found outside that plan. The couples we interviewed who were not churchgoers to a person expressed sadness that they'd not been able to find an answer within the structure of an organized church. All of them seemed to hope that some day their situation could be resolved.

Just as the two-paycheck lifestyle is not a momentary fad that will evaporate tomorrow, neither are churches. We are confident that churches will continue to be a force in society, despite angry barbs and critical comments that are often hurled at them. National Council of Churches research shows that 133,469,690 of the 226 million Americans in 1981 were affiliated with some church. That is nearly 60 percent of the population! Each year the percentage of church members in this country increases slightly—and these increases continue in an era in which churches are trying harder than ever to clean up their rolls and make them as accurate as possible. These millions of church members are putting their money where their hearts are. In 1961, each member of a Protestant church in the United States contributed an average $69 a year to a church. In 1979 the average amount climbed to $197.44. Even taking inflation into account, the National Council of Churches research shows that the "real" amount of giving increased by 18 percent over that eighteen year span.[7]

In Houston, where we live, there are more than two thousand individual Christian congregations, ranging in membership from twenty-five to fifteen thousand. In some neighborhoods there are more churches than bars, grocery stores, or other places of business. In our hometown there are more people in church on Sunday morning than there are at all the combined professional sporting events held throughout the week. Yet no one would dare say that professional sports are dying in Houston or in any other major city in the country!

It is difficult to measure the exact impact of the church community on society in general, but it is much greater than skeptics realize. In 1960, 1976, and 1980 churches played a pivotal role in the election of American presidents. When disaster strikes anywhere in the world, churches are among the first groups to offer assistance—and such help amounts to millions of dollars each year. When Pope John Paul II visited the United States in October, 1979, he drew huge crowds of spectators. I traveled in the press corps that flew with the pope from city to city on that historic visit. I remember looking out over the sea of faces on the Boston Common, on a farm in Iowa, along Chicago streets, in front of the White House, and at Madison Square Garden—all points visited by John Paul—and thinking, "These people really do take this man and the church he leads very seriously."

Kay and I believe that God's work is alive and well on Planet Earth through the various churches he has established among us, that despite their shortcomings, churches will continue to play a key role in bettering our society. At the same time, we stand committed to continue as a two-paycheck family, resolved to make our lifestyle work within the structures of these churches. We urge others to do likewise. Our parting message to two-paycheck couples is: *stay in the church and let your influence be felt.*

## A Call to Arms for Churches

Likewise, we call upon churches to awaken to the new day that is dawning in society in regard to the two-paycheck family. This is the lifestyle of the present and the future. Statistics and common sense indicate that more and more married couples will join the ranks of the two-paycheck family in the coming years. The churches must not—they cannot—abandon these families. To fight them either covertly or overtly is to sow the seeds that will eventually cause churches to lose their influence among the largest segment of the population.

We would urge churches to look on two-paycheck families as a fertile field for ministry. This increasingly prevalent lifestyle presents the churches with a new opportunity for outreach. Karen Burton Mains writes that it is especially crucial that working women see the church as ministering to their special pressures and needs. "The church will have to create opportunities to enable the organization and intellectual abilities of its female members to be developed—or resign itself to losing them."[8]

A decade from now, we believe people will single out which churches were first to respond to the needs of the two-paycheck family in the same way congregations today are being lauded for how they developed programs for singles, the divorced, and the aging several years ago. Two-paycheck couples who are already committed to the Christian faith must not let their own churches be in a position of foot-dragging in this regard. We urge working couples to make sure their churches keep an eye on the trend of the times and act accordingly.

Churches can be powerful elements for effecting changes in society. It is impossible to study social issues of our time—such as abortion, capital punishment, war, and civil rights—without acknowledging the voice and influence some churches have had on those issues. Now the two-paycheck lifestyle presents churches with a new challenge. Either they can accept the fact that working couples are becoming the new model for families of the future, or they can oppose the lifestyle, either by confronting it directly or by complacently letting it slide by, and end up alienating the people they should be reaching with the message of Jesus Christ.

Churches also have the opportunity to assist other institutions in the community in adjusting to the coming dominant lifestyle. Schools, the medical community, and businesses—to name a few—could use the spiritual and ethical guidance churches have to offer in coming to terms with this growing family style. Churches can become models for understanding and assisting the two-paycheck family form, so that others can see how it can be done. Let churches become lighthouses for society in this regard!

But before the church can teach others how to respond to two-paycheck families, it must itself learn how to relate to them in effective ways. Churches must want to understand this new way of living and to change their programs and ways of ministering, so that they reach out without alienating working couples. A *Christianity Today* editorial asks this question, which we feel is pertinent to the church's role with the two-paycheck family: "Do we dare to be self-critical? Are we willing to scrutinize the church honestly in the light of the Word of God and to correct it by that divine standard? Or do we find ourselves slipping into the position of the Pharisees in Christ's day . . . the Pharisees who in their self-righteousness refused to be self-critical, they never took the first step in order to see their needs. If we don't recognize our needs, we never try to find their remedy."[9]

For the church and the two-paycheck family, the fields are, in the words of Jesus, "white unto harvest."

# Notes

## Chapter 1

1. U.S. Department of Labor, Bureau of Labor Statistics, *Employment in Perspective: Working Women, Fourth Quarter, 1980* (Washington, D.C., 1980).
2. U.S. Department of Labor, Bureau of Labor Statistics, *New Labor Force Projections to 1990* (Washington, D.C., 1980).
3. U.S. Department of Labor, *Employment in Perspective.*
4. Ibid.
5. U.S. Department of Labor, Bureau of Labor Statistics, *Employment in Perspective: Working Women, Summary 1980* (Washington, D.C., 1980).

## Chapter 2

1. Evelyn Kaye, *Crosscurrents: Children, Families and Religion* (New York: Clarkson N. Potter, 1980), p. 3.
2. Kenneth Chafin, "Why Go to Church?" (Sermon delivered at South Main Baptist Church, Houston, Tex., 26 September 1980).
3. Clyde Francis Lytle, ed., *Leaves of Gold* (Williamsport, Penn.: Coslett Publishing Co., 1948), p. 28.

## Chapter 3

1. "Inerrancy: Clearing Away Confusion," *Christianity Today*, 29 May 1981, pp. 12–13.
2. Ibid.
3. Quoting Ragan Courtney during interview for "Southern Baptists' Golden Couple," by Louis Moore, *Houston Chronicle*, October, 1980, sec. 3, p. 1.

4. Austin H. Stouffer, "The Ordination of Women: Yes," *Christianity Today,* 20 February 1981, pp. 12–15.

5. G. Ernest Wright, ed., *Great People of the Bible and How They Lived* (Pleasantville, N.Y.: Reader's Digest Assn., 1974), p. 404.

6. "Women's Role in Church and Family," *Christianity Today,* 20 February 1981.

7. Stouffer, "The Ordination of Women," p. 14.

## Chapter 5

1. John Claypool, "Saying Yes and Saying No" (Sermon delivered at Northminster Baptist Church, Jackson, Miss., 26 February 1978).

2. John Claypool, "What Do You Do with Your Guilt?" (Sermon delivered 15 March 1981).

## Chapter 6

1. For in-depth coverage of this interview, see Louis Moore, "Some Churches Awakening to Two-Career Families' Needs," *Houston Chronicle,* 9 February 1980, sec. 1, p. 17.

## Chapter 7

1. Barbara Kaye Greenleaf, *Help: A Handbook for Working Mothers* (New York: Thomas Y. Crowell, 1978), p. 2.

2. Jean Curtis, *Working Mothers* (New York: Doubleday, 1975), p. 30.

3. Ibid., p. 31.

4. Greenleaf, p. 3.

5. Ibid., p. 2.

6. Curtis, *Working Mothers,* p. 38.

## Chapter 8

1. Barbara Kaye Greenleaf, *Help: A Handbook for Working Mothers* (New York: Thomas Y. Crowell, 1978), p. 12.

2. Hilary Ryglewicz and Pat Koch Thaler, *Working Couples* (New York: Sovereign Bks., div. of Simon & Schuster, 1980); Cynthia Sterling Pincus, *Double Duties: An Action Plan for the Working Wife* (New York: Chatham Square Press, 1978).

# NOTES

3. Ryglewicz and Thaler, *Working Couples*, p. 41.
4. Ibid., p. 46.
5. Ibid., p. 41.
6. Peggy Jones and Pam Brace, *Sidetracked Home Executives: From Pigpen to Paradise* (Portland, Or.: Binford & Mort, 1980).
7. Greenleaf, *Help*, p. 128.
8. Kay Kuzma, *Prime Time Parenting* (New York: Rawson Wade Pubs., 1980), later published under the title, *Working Mothers* (New York: Stratford Press, 1981).
9. Floyd Thatcher and Harriett Thatcher, *Long Term Marriage* (Waco, Tex.: Word Books, 1980), p. 198.

## Chapter 9

1. Hilary Ryglewicz and Pat Koch Thaler, *Working Couples* (New York: Sovereign Bks., div. of Simon & Schuster, 1980), p. 81.
2. Urie Bronfenbrenner, "The Origins of Alienation," *Scientific American,* reprinted in Kay Kuzma, *Prime Time Parenting* (New York: Rawson Wade Pubs., 1980), p. 4.
3. This section relies heavily on Henry Biller and Dennis Meredith, *Father Power* (New York: David McKay Co., 1974).
4. Jesse Jackson, quoted in *Dads Only* (monthly newsletter for Christian fathers distributed by Paul Lewis and Ray Bruce, San Diego, Calif.), December, 1979, p. 1.
5. Howard Hovde and Louis Moore, "Families of the Bible" (unpublished manuscript in files of Louis Moore, Houston, Tex., 1978).
6. Ryglewicz and Thaler, *Working Couples*, p. 80.
7. G. Wade Rowatt, Jr. and Mary Jo Rowatt, *The Two-Career Marriage* (Philadelphia: Westminster Press, 1980), p. 45.
8. Ryglewicz and Thaler, *Working Couples*, p. 78.
9. Copies of this newsletter can be obtained by writing the following address: Paul Lewis and Ray Bruce, *Dads Only*, PO Box 20594, San Diego, CA 92120.
10. Rowatt and Rowatt, *The Two-Career Marriage*, p. 104.

## Chapter 10

1. G. Wade Rowatt, Jr. and Mary Jo Rowatt, *The Two-Career Marriage* (Philadelphia: Westminster Press, 1980), p. 107.

2. Ibid.

3. Ibid., pp. 110–111.

4. Quoted in Louis Moore, "Some Churches Awakening to Two-Career Families' Needs," *Houston Chronicle,* 9 February 1980.

5. Elton Trueblood, *The Incendiary Fellowship* (New York: Harper & Row, Pubs., 1967), pp. 77–78.

6. "Love of God Demands Love for His Church," *Christianity Today,* 17 July 1981.

7. Constant H. Jacquet, Jr., quoted in Jay Merwin, "Churches Simply Not in Financial Positions to Pick Up Programs Dropped by Reagan," *Houston Chronicle,* 1 August 1981.

8. Karen Burton Mains, "It's a Mystery to Me: Struggles with Sexual Ambiguity in the Church," *Christianity Today,* 17 July 1981.

9. "Love of God Demands Love for His Church," *Christianity Today.*